JELL-O ®

BRAND

fun and fabulous recipes

from
JELL-O ®
Gelatins & Puddings

BEEKMAN HOUSE

JELL-O® BRAND

fun and fabulous recipes

Pictured on front cover: Gelatin Trifle (see page 22)

Library of Congress Catalog Card Number: 90-60060
ISBN: 0-517-03148-5

This edition published by:
Beekman House
Distributed by Crown Publishers, Inc.
225 Park Avenue South
New York, New York 10003

Printed in Yugoslavia

h g f e d c b a

GELATIN AND PUDDING PERFECTION

For ideal results with JELL-O® Brand Gelatin and JELL-O® Pudding and Pie Filling, follow the preparation tips, general hints and serving ideas given in this section. To start, always follow basic package or recipe directions. Then use these tips to make truly perfect creations!

GELATIN TIPS

To make a mixture that is clear and uniformly set, be sure the gelatin is *completely* dissolved in boiling water or other boiling liquid before adding the cold liquid.

JELL-O Brand Gelatin and Sugar Free Gelatin can be used interchangeably in recipes.

To double a recipe, simply double the amounts of gelatin, liquid and other ingredients used, except salt, vinegar and lemon juice. For these ingredients, use just 1½ times the amount given in the recipe.

To store prepared gelatin overnight or longer, cover it to prevent drying. Always store gelatin cakes or pies in the refrigerator.

IN A HURRY

Speed up the chilling time by choosing the right containers or using one of these specially developed speed-set methods.

The container: Use metal bowls or molds rather than glass, plastic or china. Metal chills more quickly and the gelatin will be firm in less time than in glass or plastic bowls. Individual servings in small molds or serving dishes will also chill more quickly than large servings.

The ice bath method: Dissolve gelatin according to package directions. Then place the bowl of gelatin mixture in another bowl of ice and water; stir occasionally as mixture chills to ensure even thickening.

The ice cube method: Completely dissolve gelatin in ¾ cup boiling liquid (1½ cups for 8-serving size package). Combine ½ cup cold water and enough ice cubes to make 1¼ cups ice and water (1 cup cold water and enough ice cubes to make 2½ cups for 8-serving size package). Add to gelatin, stirring until slightly thickened. Remove any unmelted ice. Pour into dessert dishes or bowl. Chill. Soft-set and ready to eat in about 30 minutes. *Do not* use this method if you are going to mold the gelatin.

The blender method: Place 4-serving size package of gelatin and ¾ cup boiling liquid in blender. The volume of an 8-serving size package is too large for most blenders. Cover and blend at low speed until gelatin is completely dissolved, 30 seconds. Combine ½ cup cold water and enough ice cubes to make 1¼ cups; add to gelatin. Stir until partially melted. Blend at high speed 30 seconds. Pour into dessert dishes or bowl. Chill until set, at least 30 minutes.

THE EXTRAS

Add a special touch to your gelatin dessert or salad. Try one of these ideas.

Fruits and vegetables: Chill gelatin until it is thickened, then fold in ¾ to 1½ cups (1½ to 3 cups for 8-serving size) of fruits or vegetables. If gelatin is not thick enough, the fruits or vegetables may float or sink. Do not use fresh or frozen pineapple or kiwifruit or fresh ginger root, papaya, figs or guava. An enzyme in these fruits will prevent the gelatin from setting. These fruits are fine, however, if cooked or canned, because these processes deactivate the enzyme. Canned or fresh fruits should be drained well before adding (unless a recipe specifies otherwise). Fruit juice or syrup can be used as part of liquid called for in the recipes.

Carbonated soft drinks: Substitute carbonated soft drinks, such as cola, ginger ale, root beer or lemon- or lime-flavored mixes, for part or all of the cold water.

Fruit juice: Use fruit juice for part of the liquid—orange juice, apple juice, cranberry juice, tomato juice or canned pineapple juice. Use boiling fruit juice if replacing boiling water.

Flavoring extracts: Add flavoring extracts, such as vanilla, almond, peppermint or rum—just a touch for a flavor plus.

Wine or liqueur: Add a little wine or liqueur for a festive touch. Use 2 tablespoons of white wine, red wine, sherry or port or 1 tablespoon of creme de menthe or fruit-flavored liqueur. For an 8-serving size package, use 3 tablespoons of wine or 1½ tablespoons of liqueur.

Two gelatin flavors: Mix 2 JELL-O Brand Gelatin Flavors for a new flavor combination. Use lemon or orange with any red flavor or combine any 2 red flavors.

QUICK TRICKS

No need to settle for gelatin in the same form every time. Try these different and easy ways with JELL-O Brand Gelatin!

Whip it: Chill prepared gelatin until very thick. Then beat with rotary beater or electric mixer at medium speed until mixture is fluffy and thick and about doubled in volume. Chill until firm. To shorten the chilling time, chill gelatin until slightly thickened, then use ice bath method (see page 3) and beat in bowl set in bowl of ice and water.

Flake it: Prepare gelatin as usual, reducing cold water to ¾ cup (1½ cups for 8-serving size). Pour into shallow pan and chill until firm, about 4 hours. Break into small flakes with fork, or force through ricer or large-mesh strainer. Pile lightly in dishes, alone or with fruit or topping.

Cube it: Prepare gelatin as usual, reducing cold water to ¾ cup (1½ cups for 8-serving size). Pour into shallow pan and chill until firm, about 4 hours. Cut in cubes, using sharp knife that has been dipped into hot water. To remove cubes from pan, apply warm wet cloth to bottom of pan, then remove cubes with spatula. Or quickly dip pan in warm water and invert onto plastic wrap. Serve in glasses with cream or fruit, if desired.

Layer it: Make layers with different flavors or different types of gelatin mixtures. Chill each layer until set, but not firm, before adding the next layer. If the first layer is too firm, the layers may slip apart when unmolded. Except for the first layer, the gelatin mixtures should be cool and slightly thickened before being poured into a mold; a warm mixture could soften the layer beneath it and cause mixtures to run together.

MOLDING HOW-TOS

Gelatin desserts and salads look their most spectacular when molded. The making and the unmolding can be simple, if you follow these molding tips.

Water: Use less water when preparing the gelatin mixture if dessert or salad is to be molded. For 4-serving size package of gelatin, use ¾ cup cold water. For 8-serving size package of gelatin, use 1½ cups cold water. (This adjustment has already been made in recipes in this book that are to be molded.) This makes the mold less fragile and unmolding simpler.

The mold: Although the decoratively shaped mold is traditional, almost any metal form will work. You can use one of these pans or dishes commonly found in the home: cake pans (8- or 9-inch square or round pans), tube pans (fluted or plain), or loaf pans. Use metal mixing bowls; the nested sets give you a variety of sizes. Or use metal fruit or juice cans; to unmold, dip can in warm water, then puncture bottom of can and unmold.

Size of the mold: Determine the volume of the mold first by measuring with water. Most recipes give an indication of the size of mold needed. For clear gelatin, use a 2-cup mold for a 4-serving size package of gelatin and a 4-cup mold for an 8-serving size package of gelatin. If the mold is smaller than needed, pour the extra gelatin mixture into a separate dish and serve at another time. Do not use a mold that is too large, since it would be difficult to unmold. Either the recipe should be increased or a smaller mold should be used.

Fruits and vegetables: To arrange fruits or vegetables in molds, chill gelatin until thick, then pour about ¼ inch into mold. Arrange fruits or vegetables in a decorative pattern in gelatin. Chill until set, but not firm, then pour remaining thickened gelatin over pattern in mold.

Unmolding: First, allow gelatin to set until firm, several hours or overnight. Also, chill serving plate or individual plates on which mold will be served.

Make certain that gelatin is completely firm. It should not feel sticky on top and should not mound or move to the side if mold is tilted.

Use a small pointed knife dipped in warm water to loosen top edge. Or, moisten tips of fingers and gently pull gelatin from edge of mold.

Dip mold in warm, not hot, water, just to the rim, for about 10 seconds. Lift from water, hold upright and shake slightly to loosen gelatin. Or, gently pull gelatin from edge of mold.

Use a chilled serving plate moistened with cold water; this allows gelatin to be moved after unmolding. Place moistened plate over mold and invert. Shake slightly, then lift off mold carefully. If gelatin doesn't release easily, dip the mold in warm water again for a few seconds. If necessary, move gelatin to center of serving plate.

GELATIN CHILLING TIME CHART

In all recipes, for best results, the gelatin needs to be chilled to the proper consistency. Use this chart as a guideline to determine the desired consistency and the approximate chilling time.

When recipe says:	It means gelatin should . . .	It will take about:		Use it for . . .
		Regular set	Speed set*	
"Chill until syrupy"	be consistency of thick syrup	1 hour	3 minutes	glaze for pies, fruits
"Chill until slightly thickened"	be consistency of unbeaten egg whites	1¼ hours	5 to 6 minutes	adding creamy ingredients such as whipped topping, or when mixture will be beaten
"Chill until thickened"	be thick enough so that spoon drawn through it leaves a definite impression	1½ hours	5 to 6 minutes	adding solid ingredients such as fruits or vegetables
"Chill until set but not firm"	stick to the finger when touched and should mound or move to the side when bowl or mold is tilted	2 hours	30 minutes	layering gelatin mixtures
"Chill until firm"	not stick to finger when touched and not mound or move when mold is tilted	individual molds: at least 3 hours	1 hour	unmolding and serving
		2- to 6-cup mold: at least 4 hours	2 hours	
		8- to 12-cup mold: at least 5 hours or overnight		

*Ice cube method not recommended for molding.

PUDDING TIPS

The recipes in this book use both JELL-O Pudding and Pie Filling (cooked) and JELL-O Instant Pudding and Pie Filling. These products are not interchangeable in the recipes. Be sure to use the product called for in the recipe.

JELL-O Sugar Free Pudding and Pie Filling (cooked) and JELL-O Sugar Free Instant Pudding and Pie Filling can be substituted for their respective cooked and instant pudding mixes.

Although most recipes call for whole milk, you can substitute skim milk, reconstituted nonfat dry milk, light cream or half and half for the whole milk.

Always store prepared pudding desserts and snacks in the refrigerator.

COOKED PUDDING AND PIE FILLING

Stir mixture as it cooks. Bring mixture to a full boil. Pudding will thicken as it cools.

To avoid having a film on the cooled, cooked pudding, cover surface of hot pudding with plastic wrap, placing directly on pudding and pressing down to seal out air.

For a creamier pudding, stir before serving.

INSTANT PUDDING AND PIE FILLING

Always start with *cold* milk. Beat pudding mix slowly, not vigorously.

To prepare by the blender method, pour cold milk into blender. Add pudding mix. Cover and blend at high speed for 15 seconds. Pour at once into dessert dishes or bowl.

To prepare by the shaker method, pour cold milk into a leakproof 1 quart container (1½-quart container for 6-serving size). Add pudding mix. Cover tightly; shake vigorously for 45 seconds. Pour at once into dessert dishes or bowl. Pudding will be soft-set and ready to eat in 5 minutes.

■ ■ ■

FAMILY FAVORITES

Win rave reviews with these delicious time-tested treasures. They'll become traditions in your family, too!

Chocolate Turtle Pie

■ ■ ■

CHOCOLATE TURTLE PIE

Makes one 8- or 9-inch pie

¼ cup caramel- or butterscotch-flavored dessert topping
1 baked 8- or 9-inch pie shell, cooled
¾ cup pecan halves
1 package (4-serving size) JELL-O® Chocolate Flavor
    Pudding and Pie Filling
1¾ cups milk
1¾ cups thawed COOL WHIP® Non-Dairy Whipped Topping

Place caramel topping in small saucepan. Heat over medium heat until topping comes to a boil, stirring constantly. Pour into pie shell. Arrange pecans on topping and chill.

Combine pie filling mix and milk in medium saucepan; blend well. Cook and stir over medium heat until mixture comes to a full boil. Cool 5 minutes, stirring twice. Pour over nuts in pie shell. Cover surface with plastic wrap. Chill about 3 hours. Remove plastic wrap. Pipe whipped topping around edge of pie. Drizzle with additional topping and garnish with additional pecans, if desired.

GOLDEN SALAD

Makes about 3 cups or 6 servings

1 package (4-serving size) JELL-O® Brand Lemon or
    Orange Flavor Gelatin
½ teaspoon salt
1¼ cups boiling water
1 can (8¼ ounces) crushed pineapple in juice
1 tablespoon lemon juice or vinegar
1½ cups shredded carrots
⅓ cup chopped pecans

Dissolve gelatin and salt in boiling water. Stir in undrained pineapple and lemon juice. Chill until thickened. Stir in carrots and nuts and pour into individual molds. Chill until firm, about 3 hours. Unmold. Serve with crisp salad greens and mayonnaise, if desired.

■ ■ ■

■ ■ ■

PUDDING ICE CREAM

Makes 6 cups or 12 servings

2 cups cold light cream or half and half
1 package (4-serving size) JELL-O® Vanilla or Chocolate
    Flavor Instant Pudding and Pie Filling
3½ cups (8 ounces) COOL WHIP® Non-Dairy Whipped
    Topping, thawed

Pour cold cream into bowl. Add pudding mix. With electric mixer at low speed, beat until well blended, 1 to 2 minutes. Let stand 5 minutes. Fold in whipped topping. Pour into 2-quart covered plastic container. Freeze until firm, about 6 hours.

Toffee Crunch Pudding Ice Cream: Prepare Pudding Ice Cream as directed, using vanilla flavor pudding mix and folding in ⅔ cup crushed chocolate-covered toffee bar with the whipped topping.

Rum Raisin Pudding Ice Cream: Prepare Pudding Ice Cream as directed, using vanilla flavor pudding mix. Soak ½ cup chopped raisins in 2 tablespoons light rum; fold in with the whipped topping.

Rocky Road Pudding Ice Cream: Prepare Pudding Ice Cream as directed, using chocolate flavor pudding mix and folding in 1 cup miniature marshmallows and ½ cup chopped walnuts with the whipped topping.

Cinnamon Walnut Pudding Ice Cream: Prepare Pudding Ice Cream as directed, using vanilla flavor pudding mix and adding 2 tablespoons light brown sugar and ½ teaspoon cinnamon to the pudding mix. Add ½ cup finely chopped walnuts with the whipped topping.

Fruit Pudding Ice Cream: Prepare Pudding Ice Cream as directed, folding in 1 cup pureed fruit (strawberries, peaches or raspberries) with the whipped topping.

Chocolate Chip Pudding Ice Cream: Prepare Pudding Ice Cream as directed, using chocolate flavor pudding mix and folding in ¾ cup BAKER'S® Real Semi-Sweet Chocolate Chips with the whipped topping.

■ ■ ■

BOSTON CREAM TORTE

Makes 1 cake

 1 package (4-serving size) JELL-O® Banana Cream or
    Vanilla Flavor Pudding and Pie Filling
1¾ cups milk
 2 baked 8-inch yellow cake layers, cooled
 1 square BAKER'S® Unsweetened Chocolate
 1 tablespoon butter or margarine
¾ cup confectioners sugar
1½ tablespoons hot milk
    Dash salt

Combine pudding mix and milk in medium saucepan; blend well. Cook and stir over medium heat until mixture comes to a full boil. Cover with plastic wrap; chill. Split cake layers horizontally to make 4 thin layers. Beat pudding until creamy. Spread about ⅔ cup on each layer and stack.

Melt chocolate and butter in small saucepan over very low heat, stirring constantly. Combine sugar, hot milk and salt in bowl; add chocolate. Beat until smooth. Spread over top of cake. Chill. Store cake in refrigerator.

■ ■ ■

■ ■ ■

GINGER PINEAPPLE MOLD

Makes 5 cups or 10 servings

1 can (20 ounces) pineapple slices in juice
2 packages (4-serving size) or 1 package (8-serving size)
JELL-O® Brand Lime or Apricot Flavor Gelatin
1½ cups boiling water
1 cup ginger ale or cold water
¼ teaspoon ginger

Drain pineapple, reserving juice. Cut 4 pineapple slices in half; set aside. Cut remaining pineapple slices into chunks. Dissolve gelatin in boiling water. Add reserved juice, ginger ale and ginger. Chill until slightly thickened. Measure 1 cup of the gelatin. Arrange some of the pineapple chunks in 6-cup ring mold; top with measured gelatin. Chill until set but not firm, about 10 minutes. Fold remaining pineapple chunks into remaining gelatin; spoon over gelatin in mold. Chill until firm, about 4 hours. Unmold. Garnish with halved pineapple slices, halved cherry tomatoes and crisp greens, if desired.

THUMBPRINT COOKIES

Makes 3 dozen

1 package (4-serving size) JELL-O® Instant Pudding and
   Pie Filling, any flavor

1 package (10 ounces) pie crust mix

2 tablespoons butter or margarine, melted

4 to 5 tablespoons cold water

1 package (4 ounces) BAKER'S® GERMAN'S® Sweet
   Chocolate, broken into squares

Whole or chopped toasted nuts

Combine pudding mix and pie crust mix in medium bowl; add butter and 4 tablespoons of the water. Mix with fork until soft dough forms. (If dough is too dry, add 1 tablespoon water.) Shape dough into 1-inch balls. Place 1 inch apart on ungreased baking sheets; press thumb deeply into center of each.

Cut each square of chocolate in half. Press 1 half into center of each cookie. Bake in preheated 350° oven for about 15 minutes or until lightly browned. Immediately press nuts lightly into chocolate centers. Remove from baking sheets and cool on wire racks.

Coconut Thumbprints: Prepare Thumbprint Cookies as directed, omitting chocolate and nuts. Mix 1⅓ cups (about) BAKER'S® ANGEL FLAKE® Coconut with ½ cup sweetened condensed milk; spoon into centers of cookies before baking.

Jam Thumbprints: Prepare Thumbprint Cookies as directed, omitting chocolate and nuts. Spoon ½ teaspoon jam into center of each cookie after baking.

Cream Cheese and Jelly Thumbprints: Prepare Thumbprint Cookies as directed, omitting chocolate and nuts. Using 1 package (3 ounces) cream cheese, softened, spoon ½ teaspoon cream cheese into center of each cookie before baking and top each with ½ teaspoon jelly after baking.

■ ■ ■

PISTACHIO CHOCOLATE CRUNCH PIE

Makes one 9-inch pie

½ cup blanched almonds

2 cups (1 pint) sour cream

2 cups cold milk

1 package (4-serving size) JELL-O® Pistachio Flavor
    Instant Pudding and Pie Filling

1 baked 9-inch pie shell, cooled

1 cup thawed COOL WHIP® Non-Dairy Whipped Topping

1 cup graham cracker or vanilla or chocolate wafer
    crumbs

1 package (4-serving size) JELL-O® Chocolate Flavor
    Instant Pudding and Pie Filling

Toast almonds in shallow pan in preheated 350° oven for 3 to 5 minutes, stirring once. Chop nuts; set aside. Place 1 cup of the sour cream and 1 cup of the milk in small bowl. Add pistachio flavor pie filling mix. With electric mixer at low speed, beat for 1 minute. Pour into pie shell. Spread whipped topping over filling; then sprinkle with nuts and crumbs.

Place remaining sour cream and remaining milk in another small bowl. Add chocolate flavor pie filling mix. With electric mixer at low speed, beat for 1 minute. Spoon over crumb layer. Chill about 4 hours. Garnish with additional whipped topping and multi-colored sprinkles, if desired.

BASIC BAVARIAN

Makes about 3½ cups or 6 servings

1 package (4-serving size) JELL-O® Brand Gelatin, any
    flavor

1 cup boiling water

1 cup cold water

2 cups thawed COOL WHIP® Non-Dairy Whipped Topping

Dissolve gelatin in boiling water. Add cold water. Chill until slightly thickened. Fold in 1½ cups of the whipped topping. Spoon into dessert glasses or 4-cup mold. Chill until firm, about 4 hours. (Unmold, if necessary.) Garnish with remaining whipped topping and fresh or canned fruit, if desired.

■ ■ ■

■ ■ ■

BANANA LAYERED PIE

Makes one 9-inch pie

2¼ cups cold milk

1 package (6-serving size) JELL-O® Vanilla Flavor Instant
Pudding and Pie Filling

1 baked 9-inch pie shell or prepared graham cracker crumb
crust, cooled

2 medium bananas

½ cup thawed COOL WHIP® Non-Dairy Whipped Topping
Lemon juice

Pour cold milk into bowl. Add pie filling mix. With electric mixer at low speed, beat until blended, about 1 minute. Pour ½ cup of the pie filling into pie shell.

Slice 1 banana; arrange slices on filling in shell. Top with ¾ cup of the pie filling.

Blend whipped topping into remaining pie filling. Spread over filling in pie shell. Chill about 3 hours. Slice remaining banana; brush with lemon juice. Arrange banana slices on pie. Garnish with additional whipped topping, if desired.

CREAMY PEACH SALAD

Makes about 3½ cups or 6 to 7 servings

- 1 package (4-serving size) JELL-O® Brand Peach Flavor Gelatin
- 1 cup boiling water
- ⅓ cup cold water
- ½ cup plain yogurt
- 1¾ cups thawed COOL WHIP® Non-Dairy Whipped Topping
- 1 can (16 ounces) sliced peaches, drained and chopped
- ¼ cup chopped nuts

Dissolve gelatin in boiling water. Add cold water. Chill until slightly thickened. Blend yogurt into whipped topping; then blend in gelatin. Stir in peaches and nuts. Pour into 8×4-inch loaf pan. Chill until firm, about 3 hours. Unmold. Garnish with additional peach slices, if desired.

■ ■ ■

■ ■ ■

CHIFFON PARFAITS

Makes 3½ cups or 7 servings

1 cup sliced fresh or thawed frozen strawberries, drained
¾ cup boiling water
1 package (4-serving size) JELL-O® Brand Strawberry
  Flavor Sugar Free Gelatin
½ cup cold water
  Ice cubes
1 cup thawed COOL WHIP® Non-Dairy Whipped Topping
½ teaspoon almond extract

Spoon strawberries into parfait glasses. Pour boiling water into blender. Add gelatin. Cover and blend at low speed until gelatin is completely dissolved, about 30 seconds. Combine cold water and ice cubes to make 1¼ cups. Add to gelatin and stir until ice is partially melted. Then add whipped topping and almond extract. Blend at high speed for 30 seconds. Pour over berries in glasses. Chill until set, about 30 minutes.

Raspberry Chiffon Parfaits: Prepare Chiffon Parfaits as directed, substituting 1 cup fresh raspberries and triple berry flavor gelatin for the strawberries and strawberry flavor gelatin.

VEGETABLE YOGURT SALAD

Makes 2½ cups or 5 servings

1 package (4-serving size) JELL-O® Brand Lemon Flavor
  Sugar Free Gelatin
1 cup boiling water
1 tablespoon vinegar
1 container (8 ounces) plain yogurt
1 cup grated carrots
½ cup chopped green pepper
1 tablespoon chopped chives

Dissolve gelatin in boiling water. Add vinegar. Chill until slightly thickened. Blend in yogurt; then fold in carrots, green pepper and chives. Pour into 2½- or 3-cup mold. Chill until firm, about 3 hours. Unmold. Garnish with celery leaves and carrot curls, if desired.

■ ■ ■

■ ■ ■

OLD-FASHIONED BREAD PUDDING

Makes about 4 cups or 6 servings

1 package (4-serving size) JELL-O® Vanilla Flavor Pudding
   and Pie Filling
¼ cup sugar
3 cups milk
¼ cup raisins
2 tablespoons grated lemon rind (optional)
1 tablespoon butter or margarine
½ teaspoon vanilla
6 slices dry white bread, cut into cubes
¼ teaspoon cinnamon
⅛ teaspoon nutmeg

Combine pudding mix and 2 tablespoons of the sugar in medium saucepan. Add 2 cups of the milk; blend well. Add raisins and lemon rind. Cook and stir over medium heat until mixture comes to a full boil. Remove from heat; stir in butter and vanilla.

Pour remaining milk over bread cubes in bowl to moisten; then stir into pudding mixture. Pour into 1-quart baking dish. Combine remaining sugar with spices. Sprinkle over pudding. Broil until sugar is lightly browned and bubbly, 4 to 5 minutes. Serve warm or chilled. Garnish with lemon slice, if desired.

SOUTHERN BANANA PUDDING

Makes 12 servings

1 package (6-serving size) JELL-O® Vanilla or Banana
   Cream Flavor Pudding and Pie Filling
3¾ cups milk
3 eggs, separated
2½ dozen vanilla wafers
2 large bananas, sliced
Dash salt
⅓ cup sugar

CONTINUED

■ ■ ■

. . .

Combine pudding mix, milk and egg yolks in medium saucepan; blend well. Cook and stir over medium heat until mixture comes to a full boil; set aside.

Arrange layer of vanilla wafers in bottom of 2-quart baking dish. Place a layer of banana slices over wafers in dish. Spoon a layer of pudding over bananas. Continue layering wafers, bananas and pudding, ending with pudding.

With electric mixer at medium speed, beat egg whites with salt until foamy. Gradually beat in sugar. Beat at high speed until mixture forms stiff shiny peaks. Lightly pile meringue on pudding, sealing edges well. Bake in preheated 425° oven for 5 to 10 minutes or until meringue is lightly browned. Serve warm or chilled.

Clockwise from top left: Southern Banana Pudding,
Fruit Crisp (see page 20), Old-Fashioned Bread Pudding

■ ■ ■

FRUIT CRISP

Makes about 3¼ cups or 6 servings

    5 slices white bread
    ¼ cup butter or margarine
    2 tablespoons sugar
    1 can (16 to 17 ounces) sliced peaches or fruit cocktail
    1 package (4-serving size) JELL-O® Lemon Flavor Instant
       Pudding and Pie Filling
    ⅛ teaspoon cinnamon
    ⅛ teaspoon nutmeg
    1 cup water

Toast bread and cut into ½-inch cubes. Melt butter in large skillet over medium heat. Add bread cubes and sugar. Cook and stir over medium heat until bread is evenly browned and butter mixture is absorbed; set aside.

Drain fruit, reserving ⅓ cup of the syrup. Blend pudding mix with spices in bowl. Add water and reserved syrup. Stir or beat until mixture is well blended and starts to thicken, about 1 minute; stir in fruit. Pour into serving bowl or individual dessert dishes. Top with bread cubes. Sprinkle with confectioners sugar, if desired. Let stand 15 minutes before serving.

GERMAN SWEET CHOCOLATE PIE

Makes one 9-inch pie

    1 unbaked 9-inch pie shell
    ⅓ cup butter or margarine
    ⅓ cup packed brown sugar
    ⅓ cup chopped pecans
    ⅓ cup BAKER'S® ANGEL FLAKE® Coconut
    1 package (6-serving size) JELL-O® Vanilla Flavor Pudding
       and Pie Filling
    1 package (4 ounces) BAKER'S® GERMAN'S® Sweet
       Chocolate, broken in pieces
 2½ cups milk
    1 cup thawed COOL WHIP® Non-Dairy Whipped Topping

CONTINUED

■ ■ ■

■ ■ ■

Prick pie shell thoroughly with fork. Bake in preheated 425° oven for 5 to 8 minutes or until shell begins to brown. Remove from oven.

Meanwhile, combine butter, brown sugar, nuts and coconut in medium saucepan. Heat over medium heat until butter and sugar are melted, stirring occasionally. Spread in bottom of hot pie shell. Return to 425° oven for 5 minutes or until bubbly; cool.

Combine pie filling mix, chocolate and milk in medium saucepan. Cook and stir over medium heat until mixture comes to a full boil. Remove from heat and beat to blend, if necessary. Cool 5 minutes, stirring twice. Pour over coconut mixture in pie shell. Cover surface with plastic wrap. Chill about 4 hours. Before serving, remove plastic wrap. Garnish with whipped topping and sprinkle with additional coconut, if desired.

CITRUS FRAPPÉ

Makes 3 cups or 6 servings

¾ cup boiling water
1 package (4-serving size) JELL-O® Brand Lemon, Lime or Orange Flavor Sugar Free Gelatin*
½ cup cold water
 ice cubes
½ cup lemon sherbet*

Pour boiling water into blender. Add gelatin. Cover and blend at low speed until gelatin is completely dissolved, about 30 seconds. Combine cold water and ice cubes to make 1¼ cups. Add to gelatin and stir until ice is partially melted. Add sherbet and blend at high speed for 30 seconds. Spoon into dessert dishes. Chill until set, about 15 minutes.

*Additional Flavor Combinations
Use lemon flavor gelatin with lime or raspberry sherbet.

Use orange flavor gelatin with orange sherbet.

■ ■ ■

■ ■ ■

CHERRIES JUBILEE SALAD

Makes about 5⅔ cups or 8 to 10 servings

- 1 can (20 ounces) pineapple chunks in juice
- 2 cans (6 ounces each) pineapple juice
- 2 packages (4-serving size) or 1 package (8-serving size)
  JELL-O® Brand Cherry Flavor Gelatin
- ½ cup red wine or water
- ½ teaspoon nutmeg
- 1 package (12 ounces) frozen dark sweet cherries,
  thawed
- ½ cup chopped pecans

Drain pineapple, reserving juice. Combine reserved juice and the 2 cans pineapple juice in small saucepan. Bring to a boil over high heat. Dissolve gelatin in juice. Add wine and nutmeg. Chill until slightly thickened. Fold in pineapple, cherries and pecans. Pour into 1½-quart mold. Chill until firm, about 6 hours. Unmold onto crisp salad greens, if desired.

GELATIN TRIFLE

Makes 5½ cups or 10 servings

- 1 package (4-serving size) JELL-O® Brand Strawberry
  Flavor Gelatin
- ¾ cup boiling water
- ½ cup cold water
  Ice cubes
- 1 cup sliced strawberries
- 1 cup sliced bananas
- 2 cups ½-inch pound cake cubes
- ¼ cup orange juice
- 1½ cups cold milk
- 1 package (4-serving size) JELL-O® Vanilla Flavor Instant
  Pudding and Pie Filling
- ½ cup thawed COOL WHIP® Non-Dairy Whipped Topping

CONTINUED

■ ■ ■

Completely dissolve gelatin in boiling water. Combine cold water and ice cubes to make 1¼ cups. Add to gelatin, stirring until slightly thickened. Remove any unmelted ice. Stir in strawberries and bananas. Place cake cubes in large serving bowl; sprinkle with orange juice. Spoon gelatin mixture over cake in bowl. Chill 10 to 15 minutes.

Meanwhile, pour cold milk into mixing bowl. Add pudding mix. With electric mixer at low speed, beat until well blended, 1 to 2 minutes. Let stand a few minutes to thicken. Fold in whipped topping. Spoon over gelatin in bowl. Chill. Garnish with additional whipped topping, strawberry slices and banana slices brushed with lemon juice, if desired.

■ ■ ■

■ ■ ■

LAYERED COOKIE PUDDING

Makes about 3 cups or 5 to 6 servings

4 cookies, coarsely crumbled
1 cup thawed COOL WHIP® Non-Dairy Whipped Topping
2 cups cold milk
1 package (4-serving size) JELL-O® Instant Pudding and
    Pie Filling, any flavor

Gently fold cookies into whipped topping. Pour cold milk into bowl. Add pudding mix. With electric mixer at low speed, beat until well blended, 1 to 2 minutes. Pour half of the pudding into individual dessert glasses. Spoon 3 to 4 tablespoons of the whipped topping mixture over pudding in glasses. Spoon remaining pudding over whipped topping mixture. Garnish with additional whipped topping and halved cookies or whole strawberries, if desired.

POUND CAKE

Makes two 9 × 5-inch loaves

1 package (2-layer size) yellow cake mix or pudding-
    included cake mix
1 package (4-serving size) JELL-O® Vanilla, Butterscotch,
    Butter Pecan or Lemon Flavor Pudding and Pie Filling
1 cup (½ pint) sour cream or plain yogurt
⅓ cup vegetable oil
4 eggs
⅛ to ¼ teaspoon mace (optional)

Combine all ingredients in large bowl. With electric mixer at low speed, blend just to moisten, scraping sides of bowl often. Then beat at medium speed for 4 minutes. Pour batter into 2 greased and floured 9×5-inch loaf pans. Bake in preheated 350° oven for 40 to 45 minutes or until cake tester inserted in center of cakes comes out clean and cakes begin to pull away from sides of pans. Cool in pans on wire rack 15 minutes. Remove from pans and finish cooling on wire racks. Sprinkle with confectioners sugar, if desired.

■ ■ ■

Pound Cake

■ ■ ■

PUDDING CHEESE PIE

Makes one 9-inch pie

1 package (8 ounces) cream cheese, softened
2 cups cold milk
1 package (4-serving size) JELL-O® Lemon, Coconut
    Cream, Vanilla or Pineapple Cream Flavor Instant
    Pudding and Pie Filling
1 prepared 9-inch graham cracker crumb crust or baked
    pie shell, cooled

With electric mixer at low speed, beat cream cheese until very soft. Gradually add ½ cup of the milk, beating until smooth. Add remaining milk and the pie filling mix, beating at low speed until blended, 1 minute. Pour immediately into pie crust. Chill until firm, about 2 hours. Sprinkle with nutmeg, if desired.

Sour Cream Cheese Pie: Prepare Pudding Cheese Pie as directed, using lemon flavor pudding and pie filling and substituting 1 cup sour cream for 1 cup of the milk.

Deluxe Lemon Pudding Cheese Pie: Prepare Pudding Cheese Pie as directed, using lemon flavor pudding and pie filling, increasing cream cheese to 11 to 12 ounces and adding 2 tablespoons sugar and ½ teaspoon vanilla with pie filling mix before beating.

Strawberry Almond Cheese Pie: Combine 1 cup sliced fresh strawberries, ¼ cup chopped toasted almonds and 1 tablespoon sugar. Spread in bottom of pie crust. Prepare Pudding Cheese Pie as directed, using vanilla flavor pudding and pie filling. Pour over strawberry mixture in pie crust. Garnish with whipped topping and additional strawberries, if desired.

Strawberry Cheese Pie: Prepare Pudding Cheese Pie as directed, using vanilla flavor pudding and pie filling, reducing milk to 1½ cups and folding in 1 cup sliced fresh strawberries. If desired, add a few drops of red food coloring to pie filling mixture before pouring into pie crust. Garnish with additional sliced strawberries, if desired.

Spicy Pudding Cheese Pie: Prepare Pudding Cheese Pie as directed, adding ¼ teaspoon cinnamon and ¼ teaspoon nutmeg.

Jelly Cheese Pie: Prepare Pudding Cheese Pie as directed, spreading about ½ cup jelly or jam on bottom of pie crust before pouring in filling.

Banana Pudding Cheese Pie: Prepare Pudding Cheese Pie as directed, adding 1 sliced banana to pie filling mixture before pouring into pie crust.

■ ■ ■

■ ■ ■

GARDEN VEGETABLE SALAD

Makes about 2 cups or 4 servings

1 package (4-serving size) JELL-O® Brand Sugar Free
   Lemon Flavor Gelatin
½ teaspoon salt
1 cup boiling water
¾ cup cold water
1 tablespoon vinegar
½ cup sliced radishes
1 tablespoon sliced scallions

Dissolve gelatin and salt in boiling water. Add cold water and vinegar. Chill until slightly thickened. Stir in radishes and scallions. Pour into individual molds. Chill until firm, about 3 hours. Unmold. Garnish with escarole, sliced hard-cooked eggs and whole radishes, if desired.

GELATIN HEAVENLY HASH

Makes 4 cups or 8 servings

1 package (4-serving size) JELL-O® Brand Gelatin, any
   flavor
¾ cup boiling water
½ cup cold water
   Ice cubes
1 cup thawed COOL WHIP® Non-Dairy Whipped Topping or
   sour cream
1 can (20 ounces) crushed pineapple, drained
1 can (11 ounces) mandarin orange sections, drained
1 cup miniature marshmallows
¼ cup chopped walnuts or pecans

Completely dissolve gelatin in boiling water. Combine cold water and ice cubes to make 1¼ cups. Add to gelatin, stirring until slightly thickened. Remove any unmelted ice. Add whipped topping, blending until smooth. Stir in pineapple, mandarin oranges, marshmallows and nuts. Pour into serving bowl or individual dessert dishes. Chill until set, about 2 hours. Garnish with additional fruits and mint leaves, if desired.

■ ■ ■

■ ■ ■

PUDDING MOUSSE

Makes 2⅔ cups or 5 servings

1½ cups cold milk
1 package (4-serving size) JELL-O® Sugar Free Instant Pudding and Pie Filling, any flavor
1 cup thawed COOL WHIP® Non-Dairy Whipped Topping

Pour cold milk into bowl. Add pudding mix. With electric mixer at low speed, beat until well blended, 1 to 2 minutes. Fold in whipped topping and spoon into dessert glasses. Garnish with additional whipped topping, if desired.

Coffee Mousse: Prepare Pudding Mousse as directed, using vanilla or chocolate flavor instant pudding and pie filling and adding 2 teaspoons MAXWELL HOUSE® or YUBAN® Instant Coffee with the pudding mix.

Lemon Mousse: Prepare Pudding Mousse as directed, using vanilla flavor instant pudding and pie filling and adding 1½ teaspoons grated lemon rind with the whipped topping.

■ ■ ■

BANANA SPLIT PIE

Makes one 9-inch pie

    2 cups cold milk
    1 package (4-serving size) JELL-O® Chocolate Flavor
       Instant Pudding and Pie Filling
 1¾ cups thawed COOL WHIP® Non-Dairy Whipped Topping
    1 baked 9-inch pie shell, cooled
    1 medium banana, sliced
    1 package (4-serving size) JELL-O® Vanilla Flavor Instant
       Pudding and Pie Filling
    2 squares BAKER'S® Semi-Sweet Chocolate, melted

Pour 1 cup of the cold milk into bowl. Add chocolate flavor pie filling mix. With electric mixer at low speed, beat until blended, about 1 minute. Fold in 1 cup of the whipped topping. Pour into pie shell; top with banana slices.

Pour remaining cold milk into another bowl. Add vanilla flavor pie filling mix. With electric mixer at low speed, beat until blended, about 1 minute. Fold in remaining whipped topping. Pour over bananas in pie shell. Freeze or chill about 4 hours. Just before serving, drizzle with melted chocolate. Garnish with additional whipped topping and stemmed maraschino cherries, if desired.

GELATIN POKE LAYER CAKE

Makes one 8- or 9-inch cake

    2 baked 8- or 9-inch white cake layers, cooled
    2 packages (4-serving size) or 1 package (8-serving size)
       JELL-O® Brand Gelatin, any flavor
    2 cups boiling water
 3½ cups (8 ounces) COOL WHIP® Non-Dairy Whipped
       Topping, thawed

Place cake layers, top-side up, in 2 clean 8- or 9-inch cake pans. Prick each cake with utility fork at ½-inch intervals. Dissolve gelatin in boiling water. Carefully spoon over cake layers. Chill 3 to 4 hours. Dip 1 cake pan in warm water for 10 seconds; then unmold onto serving plate. Top with about 1 cup of the whipped topping. Unmold second cake layer and carefully place on first layer. Frost top and sides with remaining whipped topping. Chill.

■ ■ ■

MARVELOUS SNACKS

These delectable munchies are quick to make and are ideal for after-school treats and late-night refrigerator raids.

Peanut Butter Snacking Cups

■ ■ ■

Peanut Butter Snacking Cups

Makes 12 servings

¾ cup graham cracker crumbs

3 tablespoons butter or margarine, melted

3½ cups (8 ounces) COOL WHIP® Non-Dairy Whipped
Topping, thawed

1 cup milk

½ cup chunky peanut butter

1 package (4-serving size) JELL-O® Vanilla Flavor Instant
Pudding and Pie Filling

¼ cup strawberry preserves

Line 12-cup muffin pan with paper baking cups. Combine crumbs and butter; mix well. Press about 1 tablespoon of the crumb mixture into each cup. Top each with about 1 tablespoon of the whipped topping. Gradually add milk to peanut butter in bowl, blending until smooth. Add pudding mix. With electric mixer at low speed, beat until blended, 1 to 2 minutes. Fold in remaining whipped topping. Spoon into crumb-lined cups. Top each cup with 1 teaspoon of the preserves. Freeze about 4 hours. To serve, peel off papers.

Fluffy Ice Cream Dessert

Makes 2½ cups or 5 servings

1 cup sliced or diced fresh fruit*

¾ cup boiling water

1 package (4-serving size) JELL-O® Brand Gelatin, any
flavor

½ cup ice cubes

1 cup (½ pint) vanilla ice cream

Spoon fruit into individual dessert dishes. Pour boiling water into blender. Add gelatin. Cover and blend at low speed until gelatin is completely dissolved, about 30 seconds. Add ice cubes and stir until ice is partially melted. Add ice cream and blend at high speed for 30 seconds. Pour mixture over fruit in dessert dishes. Chill until soft-set, 5 minutes.

*Do not use fresh pineapple, kiwifruit, mango, papaya or figs.

■ ■ ■

■ ■ ■

LUSCIOUS FRUITY SUNDAE

Makes 4 servings

- 1 package (4-serving size) JELL-O® Brand Gelatin, any flavor
- ¾ cup boiling water
- ½ cup cold water
  Ice cubes
- 2 cups (1 pint) ice cream, any flavor
- ½ cup fruit sundae sauce or drained fruit (optional)
- 1 cup thawed COOL WHIP® Non-Dairy Whipped Topping
- ¼ cup chopped nuts (optional)
- 4 stemmed maraschino cherries

Completely dissolve gelatin in boiling water. Combine cold water and ice cubes to make 1¼ cups. Add to gelatin, stirring until slightly thickened. Remove any unmelted ice. Alternately spoon ice cream and gelatin into tall sundae glasses, ending with gelatin and filling to within ½ inch of the top of the glass. Top with sauce, whipped topping, nuts and a cherry.

FROZEN PUDDING SANDWICHES

Makes 12 sandwiches

- 1½ cups cold milk
- ½ cup peanut butter (optional)*
- 1 package (4-serving size) JELL-O® Instant Pudding and Pie Filling, any flavor
- 24 graham cracker squares*

Gradually add milk to peanut butter in bowl, blending until smooth. Add pudding mix. With electric mixer at low speed, beat until well blended, 1 to 2 minutes. Let stand 5 minutes. Spread filling about ½ inch thick on 12 of the graham cracker squares. Top with remaining squares, pressing lightly and smoothing around edges with spatula. Freeze until firm, about 3 hours. Sandwiches can be stored, wrapped, in freezer 3 to 4 days.

*When omitting peanut butter, reduce squares to 18; makes 9 sandwiches.

■ ■ ■

Luscious Fruity Sundae

■ ■ ■

STRAWBERRIES AND CREAM

Makes about 4 cups or 8 servings

2 cups cold milk

1 package (6-serving size) JELL-O® Vanilla Flavor Instant Pudding and Pie Filling

1 teaspoon vanilla

2 cups thawed COOL WHIP® Non-Dairy Whipped Topping

2 packages (10 ounces each) BIRDS EYE® Quick Thaw Strawberries in a Lite Syrup, thawed and drained

Pour cold milk into bowl. Add pudding mix and vanilla. With electric mixer at low speed, beat until well blended, 1 to 2 minutes. Fold in whipped topping. Chill 20 minutes or until pudding mixture is thick. Layer pudding mixture and strawberries in individual dessert dishes. Chill.

FROZEN CHOCOLATE GRAHAM CUPS

Makes about 4 cups or 8 servings

1½ cups cold milk

1 package (4-serving size) JELL-O® Chocolate Flavor Instant Pudding and Pie Filling

1 cup thawed COOL WHIP® Non-Dairy Whipped Topping

7 whole graham crackers, broken in pieces

½ cup miniature marshmallows

¼ cup chopped salted peanuts

Pour cold milk into bowl. Add pudding mix. With electric mixer at low speed, beat until well blended, 1 to 2 minutes. Let stand 5 minutes. Fold in whipped topping, crackers, marshmallows and peanuts. Spoon into muffin pan lined with paper baking cups. Freeze until firm, about 3 hours. Garnish with additional whipped topping, if desired.

Frozen Vanilla Graham Cups: Prepare Frozen Chocolate Graham Cups as directed, substituting vanilla flavor instant pudding and pie filling for the chocolate flavor pudding and ¼ cup chopped nuts or slivered almonds and ¼ cup diced maraschino cherries for the marshmallows and peanuts. Makes 3 cups or 6 servings.

■ ■ ■

MELON WEDGES

Makes 6 servings

1 cantaloupe or honeydew melon

1 package (4-serving size) JELL-O® Brand Apricot or
   Orange Flavor Sugar Free Gelatin

1 cup boiling water

¾ cup cold water

1 banana, sliced, ½ cup sliced strawberries or 1 can
   (8¼ ounces) crushed pineapple in juice, well drained

Cut melon in half lengthwise; scoop out seeds and drain well. Dissolve gelatin in boiling water. Add cold water. Chill until slightly thickened. Stir in fruit. Pour into melon halves. Chill until firm, about 3 hours. Cut in wedges. Serve with additional fresh fruit, cottage cheese and crisp greens, if desired.

Note: Chill any excess fruited gelatin in dessert dish.

■ ■ ■

• • •

CHERRY WALDORF SNACK

Makes 2½ cups or 5 servings

- 1 package (4-serving size) JELL-O® Brand Cherry Flavor Gelatin
  Dash salt
- ¾ cup boiling water or apple juice
- ½ cup cold water or apple juice
  Ice cubes
- ½ cup diced peeled pear or apple
- 1 small banana, sliced or diced
- ¼ cup sliced celery or chopped nuts

Completely dissolve gelatin and salt in boiling water. Combine cold water and ice cubes to make 1¼ cups. Add to gelatin, stirring until slightly thickened. Remove any unmelted ice. Fold in fruits and celery. Spoon into bowl or individual dishes. Chill until set, about 2 hours. Garnish with additional fresh fruit and celery leaves, if desired.

■ ■ ■

CITRUS SORBET

Makes 3 cups or 6 servings

1 package (4-serving size) JELL-O® Brand Lemon, Lime or
   Orange Flavor Gelatin
1¼ cups boiling water
1 cup ice cubes
¾ cup light corn syrup or ½ cup sugar
1 tablespoon lemon, lime or orange juice
1 tablespoon lemon, lime or orange rind
2 egg whites, unbeaten, or 1 whole egg, slightly beaten*

Completely dissolve gelatin in boiling water. Add ice cubes, stirring until ice is melted. Stir in remaining ingredients. Pour into 13×9-inch pan. Freeze until partially frozen, about 2 hours.

Spoon half of the mixture into blender or food processor. Cover and process until smooth but not melted, about 30 seconds. Pour into 1½-quart plastic container. Repeat procedure with remaining mixture. Cover and freeze until firm, about 6 hours.

*Use only clean eggs with no cracks in shell.

FROZEN PUDDING

Makes 2⅓ cups or 4 servings

1 cup cold milk
1 cup cold heavy cream or milk
1 package (4-serving size) JELL-O® Instant Pudding and
   Pie Filling, any flavor*
1 to 2 tablespoons sugar*

Pour cold milk and cold heavy cream into bowl. Add pudding mix and sugar. With electric mixer at low speed, beat until just blended, about 1 minute. Pour into shallow pan and freeze until firm, about 4 hours. Let stand at room temperature 15 minutes before serving.

Note: Mixture may also be poured into 8×4-inch loaf pan and frozen until firm, about 6 hours. Unmold and slice to serve.

*With coconut cream flavor instant pudding and pie filling, omit sugar.

■ ■ ■

■ ■ ■

JIGGLERS

Makes about 8 dozen cubes or 3 dozen cutouts

4 packages (4-serving size) or 2 packages (8-serving size)
JELL-O® Brand Gelatin or Sugar Free Gelatin, any
flavor

2½ cups boiling water or fruit juice

Completely dissolve gelatin in boiling water or juice. Pour into 13×9-inch pan. Chill until firm, about 3 hours. To remove, dip pan in warm water, about 15 seconds. Cut into 1-inch squares or use cookie cutter to cut decorative shapes. Cut remaining gelatin into cubes.

Notes: For thicker Jigglers, use an 8- or 9-inch square pan.

CONTINUED

To use ice cube trays, pour gelatin mixture into 2 to 3 ice cube trays. Chill until firm, about 2 hours. To remove, dip trays in warm water, about 15 seconds. Moisten tips of fingers and gently pull Jigglers from edges.

Jigglers with Dip: Prepare Jigglers as directed. Cut as desired. Serve with assorted fruit as dippers for whipped topping or other fruit dips.

Jiggler Kabobs: Prepare Jigglers as directed. Cut into 1-inch squares. Place squares on skewers alternately with large marshmallows, whole strawberries and sliced bananas. Makes 12 to 15 kabobs.

Fruited Jigglers: Prepare Jigglers as directed. Pour into 9-inch square pan. Arrange banana slices, pineapple chunks or strawberry slices in gelatin so that when cubes are cut, each will contain one piece of fruit. Chill until firm. Cut into cubes.

JELLIED CUTOUTS

Makes 8 servings

 1 **package (4-serving size) JELL-O® Brand Gelatin, any red flavor**
1½ **cups boiling water**
 1 **package (4-serving size) JELL-O® Brand Lemon Flavor Gelatin**
 1 **cup boiling water**
 1 **cup cold water**

Completely dissolve red flavor gelatin in 1½ cups boiling water. Pour into 9-inch square pan. Chill until firm, about 3 hours. To remove, dip pan in warm water, about 15 seconds. Use cookie cutters to cut decorative shapes. Carefully transfer cutouts to 8 shallow dessert dishes. Cut remaining gelatin into cubes.

Meanwhile, dissolve lemon flavor gelatin in 1 cup boiling water. Add cold water. Chill until slightly thickened. Pour around the cutouts in dishes. Chill until set, about 3 hours.

■ ■ ■

GLAZED POPCORN

Makes 2 quarts

- 8 cups popped popcorn
- ¼ cup butter or margarine
- 3 tablespoons light corn syrup
- ½ cup packed light brown sugar or granulated sugar
- 1 package (4-serving size) JELL-O® Brand Gelatin, any flavor

Place popcorn in large bowl. Heat butter and syrup in small saucepan over low heat. Stir in brown sugar and gelatin; bring to a boil over medium heat. Reduce heat to low and gently simmer for 5 minutes. Pour syrup immediately over popcorn, tossing to coat well. Spread popcorn on aluminum-foil-lined 15×10×1-inch pan, using two forks to spread evenly. Bake in preheated 300° oven for 10 minutes. Cool. Remove from pan and break into small pieces.

Rainbow Popcorn: Prepare Glazed Popcorn 3 times, using 3 different gelatin colors, such as strawberry, lemon and lime. Bake as directed and break into pieces. Layer 3 cups of each variety in 3-quart bowl. Serve remaining popcorn at another time. Makes 6 quarts.

FRUIT JUICE CUBES

Makes 4 servings

- 1 package (4-serving size) JELL-O® Brand Gelatin, any flavor
- ¾ cup boiling water
- 1 cup apple, orange, grape, grapefruit or canned pineapple juice

Dissolve gelatin in boiling water. Add fruit juice. Pour into 8- or 9-inch square pan. Chill until firm, about 3 hours. Then cut into cubes, using sharp knife that has been dipped in hot water. Serve with fruit or on lettuce, if desired.

Note: For thicker cubes, use 8×4-inch or 9×5-inch loaf pan or double recipe and use 8- or 9-inch square pan.

■ ■ ■

···

GELATIN BANANA SPLITS

Makes 3 or 4 servings

    1 package (4-serving size) JELL-O® Brand Gelatin, any
       flavor
    1 cup boiling water
    1 cup cold water
3 or 4 medium bananas
       Lemon juice
    ½ cup thawed COOL WHIP® Non-Dairy Whipped Topping
3 or 4 maraschino cherries
       Chopped nuts

Dissolve gelatin in boiling water. Add cold water and pour into deep narrow bowl. Chill until firm. Just before serving, cut bananas in half lengthwise; brush with lemon juice and arrange in banana-split dishes. Scoop gelatin onto bananas. Garnish with whipped topping, cherries and nuts.

■ ■ ■

GELATIN FRUIT BOUQUET

Makes about 4 cups or 8 servings

1 jar (16 or 17 ounces) fruits for salad
   Chives or scallions
2 packages (4-serving size) or 1 package (8-serving size)
   JELL-O® Brand Orange Flavor Gelatin
1 cup cold water
   Ice cubes

Drain fruit, reserving syrup. Add water to syrup to make 1½ cups. Arrange fruit on bottom of 9-inch cake pan, using pear pieces to resemble woven basket. Cut peaches into pieces to make daffodils and use cherries for center of flowers. Use either chives or scallions for stems.

Place measured liquid in small saucepan. Bring to a boil over high heat. Completely dissolve gelatin in boiling liquid. Combine cold water and ice cubes to make 2½ cups. Add to gelatin, stirring until slightly thickened. Remove any unmelted ice. Measure 1 cup of the gelatin; pour into another 9-inch cake pan. Quickly transfer arrangement of fruits onto gelatin. Carefully spoon remaining gelatin over fruit. Chill overnight. Unmold. Serve with any remaining fruit.

Note: Fruits may be arranged to resemble a face or decorative pattern.

ROCKY ROAD PUDDING

Makes 3 cups or 6 servings

2 cups cold milk
1 package (4-serving size) JELL-O® Chocolate Flavor
   Instant Pudding and Pie Filling
½ cup miniature marshmallows
⅓ cup unsalted peanuts, coarsely chopped
⅓ cup BAKER'S® Real Semi-Sweet Chocolate Chips

Pour cold milk into bowl. Add pudding mix. With electric mixer at low speed, beat until well blended, 1 to 2 minutes. Let stand 5 minutes. Fold in marshmallows, peanuts and chocolate chips. Spoon into individual dessert dishes. Chill about 2 hours. Garnish with whipped topping and additional chopped peanuts, if desired.

■ ■ ■

Gelatin Fruit Bouquet

STRAWBERRY-BANANA SNACK

Makes about 2¾ cups or 4 or 5 servings

1 package (4-serving size) JELL-O® Brand Strawberry
   Flavor Gelatin
¾ cup boiling water
½ cup cold water
   Ice cubes
1 medium banana, sliced
   Mixed fresh fruit, sliced or diced

CONTINUED

■ ■ ■

■ ■ ■

Completely dissolve gelatin in boiling water. Combine cold water and ice cubes to make 1¼ cups. Add to gelatin, stirring until slightly thickened. Remove any unmelted ice. Let stand until thickened, 5 to 10 minutes. Stir in banana and pour into serving bowl. Chill until set, about 1 hour. Serve topped with mixed fresh fruit.

MUFFIN PAN SNACKS

Makes 4 cups or 8 to 10 servings

  1 **package (4-serving size) JELL-O® Brand Lemon Flavor Gelatin**
  ½ **teaspoon salt**
  ⅛ **teaspoon garlic powder**
1½ **cups boiling water**
  2 **teaspoons vinegar**
  1 **teaspoon vegetable oil**
  ⅛ **teaspoon black pepper**
  ⅛ **teaspoon dried oregano, crumbled**
     Snack combinations*

Dissolve gelatin, salt and garlic powder in boiling water. Add vinegar, oil, pepper and oregano. Place aluminum-foil baking cups in muffin pans. Place different snack combinations in each cup, filling each about ⅔ full. Then fill with gelatin mixture. Chill until firm, about 2 hours. Unmold carefully from foil cups. Serve with crisp salad greens, if desired.

*Snack Combinations
Use cauliflower florets with diced pimiento.

Use cucumber slices with tomato slices.

Use chopped hard-cooked egg with chopped cucumber and pickle.

Use shredded carrot with raisins.

Use drained canned button or sliced mushrooms with pimiento strips.

Use diced apple with chopped nuts.

Use sliced hard-cooked egg with anchovies.

Use cubed cream cheese with chopped nuts.

Use sliced celery with sliced ripe or stuffed green olives.

■ ■ ■

■ ■ ■

SHAKER ADD-IN PUDDING

Makes 2⅓ cups or 4 servings

    2 cups cold milk
    1 package (4-serving size) JELL-O® Instant Pudding and
        Pie Filling, any flavor
       Add-Ins*

Pour cold milk into 1-quart container with tight-fitting lid. Add pudding mix. Cover tightly. Holding container on top and bottom, shake hard for 45 seconds. Let stand 1 to 2 minutes. Stir in Add-Ins. Pour into individual dessert glasses. Garnish with additional Add-Ins, if desired.

*Suggested Add-Ins
Use ½ cup chocolate or butterscotch chips.

Use ½ cup raisins, coarsely chopped nuts or miniature marshmallows.

Use ½ cup crushed cookies, BAKER'S® ANGEL FLAKE® Coconut or small candies.

ORANGE FLUFF

Makes 3 cups or 6 servings

    1 can (8½ ounces) sliced peaches in juice
    ¾ cup boiling water
    1 package (4-serving size) JELL-O® Brand Orange Flavor
        Sugar Free Gelatin
       Ice cubes
    ½ cup low-fat cottage cheese
    ¼ teaspoon almond extract (optional)

Drain peaches, reserving juice. Add water to juice to make ½ cup; set aside. Dice peaches and place in individual dessert dishes. Pour boiling water into blender. Add gelatin. Cover and blend at low speed until gelatin is completely dissolved, about 30 seconds. Combine measured liquid and ice cubes to make 1¼ cups. Add to gelatin and stir until ice is partially melted. Then add cottage cheese and extract. Blend at high speed for 30 seconds. Pour over peaches in glasses. Chill until set, about 30 minutes. Garnish as desired.

■ ■ ■

■ ■ ■

Quick Pudding Cookies

Makes about 2 dozen

1 package (4-serving size) JELL-O® Instant Pudding and
    Pie Filling, any flavor
1 cup all-purpose biscuit mix
¼ cup vegetable oil
1 egg, slightly beaten
3 tablespoons water

Combine pudding mix and biscuit mix in medium bowl. Stir in oil, egg and water, blending well. Drop from teaspoon 2 inches apart onto ungreased baking sheets. Bake in preheated 375° oven for about 12 minutes, or until lightly browned. Remove from baking sheets and cool on wire racks. Store in tightly covered container.

Quick Pudding Chip Cookies: Prepare Quick Pudding Cookies as directed, stirring in ½ cup BAKER'S® Semi-Sweet Chocolate Flavored Chips just before baking. Makes 2½ dozen cookies.

Note: Cookie dough may be pressed through cookie press, or rolled into 1-inch balls and flattened on baking sheets with fork or glass dipped in flour; reduce water to 2 tablespoons.

Apple Cider Dessert

Makes 2¾ cups or 5 servings

1 package (4-serving size) JELL-O® Brand Sugar Free
    Gelatin, any flavor
¾ cup boiling water
½ cup cold apple cider or juice
    Ice cubes
1 medium unpeeled apple, cut into matchstick pieces
    (about 1½ cups)

Completely dissolve gelatin in boiling water. Combine cold cider and ice cubes to make 1¼ cups. Add to gelatin, stirring until slightly thickened. Remove any unmelted ice. Stir in apple. Pour into serving bowl or dessert dishes. Chill until set, about 1 hour. Garnish with apple slices brushed with lemon juice, if desired.

■ ■ ■

■ ■ ■

FRUITED FRUIT JUICE GELATIN

Makes 5 cups or 10 servings

2 packages (4-serving size) or 1 package (8-serving size)
    JELL-O® Brand Orange Flavor Sugar Free Gelatin*
1½ cups boiling water
  1 cup cold apple juice*
    Ice cubes
1½ cups diced apples*

Completely dissolve gelatin in boiling water. Combine cold fruit juice and ice cubes to make 2½ cups. Add to gelatin, stirring until slightly thickened. Remove any unmelted ice. Stir in apples. Pour into bowl or individual dessert glasses. Chill until set, about 4 hours. Garnish with celery leaves and additional fruit, if desired.

*Additional Flavor Combinations
Use strawberry flavor gelatin with canned pineapple juice, 1½ cups diced apples and ¼ cup chopped nuts.

Use raspberry flavor gelatin with cranberry juice cocktail, 1½ cups diced oranges, 2 tablespoons chopped nuts and ¼ cup chopped celery.

Use strawberry-banana flavor gelatin with orange juice and 1½ cups sliced bananas.

Use strawberry flavor gelatin with grape juice and 1½ cups seedless green grapes.

SNACK CUPS

Makes about 3 cups or 6 servings

1 package (4-serving size) JELL-O® Brand Orange, Lemon
    or Lime Flavor Sugar Free Gelatin
¾ cup boiling water
½ cup cold water
    Ice cubes
1 tablespoon lemon juice (optional)
½ cup each sliced celery, chopped cabbage and shredded
    carrot*

CONTINUED

■ ■ ■

■ ■ ■

Completely dissolve gelatin in boiling water. Combine cold water and ice cubes to make 1¼ cups. Add to gelatin with lemon juice, stirring until slightly thickened. Remove any unmelted ice. Fold in vegetables; spoon into individual glasses. Chill until set, about 30 minutes. Garnish with parsley, if desired.

*Additional Vegetable Combinations
Use sliced celery with grated carrots and golden raisins.

Use sliced celery with chopped cabbage, chopped apple or sliced ripe or green pitted olives.

Use sliced celery with chopped cucumber and chopped pimiento.

Use sliced celery with drained mandarin orange sections and chopped green pepper.

Ice Cream with Hot Chocolate Pudding

■ ■ ■

ICE CREAM WITH HOT CHOCOLATE PUDDING

Makes 6 to 8 servings

1 package (4-serving size) JELL-O® Chocolate Flavor
   Pudding and Pie Filling*
2 cups milk
2 cups (1 pint) vanilla or chocolate ice cream*

Combine pudding mix and milk in medium saucepan; blend well. Cook and stir over medium heat until mixture comes to a full boil. Scoop ice cream into individual dessert dishes. Immediately pour hot pudding over ice cream in dishes. Serve at once.

Note: For fewer servings, pour any remaining pudding into individual serving dishes and chill.

*Additional Flavor Combinations
Use vanilla flavor pudding mix with chocolate ice cream.

Use butterscotch flavor pudding mix with chocolate or vanilla ice cream.

Use coconut cream flavor pudding mix with vanilla ice cream.

Use banana cream flavor pudding mix with chocolate or vanilla ice cream.

MILK WHIP

Makes 3 cups or 6 servings

¾ cup boiling water
 1 package (4-serving size) JELL-O® Brand Sugar Free
    Gelatin, any flavor
½ cup cold whole milk
   Ice cubes

Pour boiling water into blender. Add gelatin. Cover and blend at low speed until gelatin is completely dissolved, about 30 seconds. Combine cold milk and ice cubes to make 1¼ cups. Add to gelatin and stir until ice is partially melted; then blend at high speed for 30 seconds. Spoon into individual dessert dishes or serving bowl. Sprinkle with cinnamon or nutmeg, if desired. Chill until set, about 30 minutes.

Banana Whip: Prepare Milk Whip as directed, adding 1 medium banana, sliced, with the milk.

■ ■ ■

EASY AND DELICIOUS

From casual to special, these fuss-free desserts or salads will be the star of any meal. And they're a snap to prepare.

Peachy Orange Ring

■ ■ ■

PEACHY ORANGE RING

Makes about 5¼ cups or 10 servings

  1 can (16 ounces) sliced peaches, drained
  2 packages (4-serving size) or 1 package (8-serving size)
    JELL-O® Brand Orange Flavor Gelatin
  2 cups boiling water
1½ cups cold water or ginger ale
  ½ cup chopped celery
  ½ cup chopped pecans

Set aside 7 peach slices; dice remaining peaches. Dissolve gelatin in boiling water. Add cold water. Measure 1¼ cups of the gelatin and pour into 6-cup fluted tube pan. Chill until set but not firm. Chill remaining gelatin until thickened. Arrange peach slices on set gelatin in pan. Gently press peaches down almost to the bottom of the pan. Chill. Add diced peaches, celery and nuts to thickened gelatin; spoon over set gelatin in pan. Chill until firm, about 4 hours. Unmold. Garnish with endive and additional peach slices, if desired.

LAYERED PINEAPPLE-CARROT SALAD

Makes about 4 cups or 8 servings

  1 can (8¼ ounces) pineapple slices, drained
  ¼ cup shredded carrot
  ¾ cup boiling water
  1 package (4-serving size) JELL-O® Brand Orange Flavor
    Gelatin
  ½ cup cold water
    Ice cubes

Cut pineapple slices in half; arrange pineapple and carrot in 8×4-inch loaf pan. Pour boiling water into blender. Add gelatin. Cover and blend at low speed until gelatin is completely dissolved, about 30 seconds. Combine cold water and ice cubes to make 1 cup. Add to gelatin and stir until ice is partially melted; then blend at high speed for 30 seconds. Pour into pan. Chill until firm, about 3 hours. Salad layers as it chills. Unmold. Garnish with chicory and carrot curls, if desired.

■ ■ ■

■ ■ ■

PUDDING IN A CLOUD

Makes about 3½ cups or 6 servings

1 **package (4-serving size) JELL-O® Pudding and Pie Filling,
    any flavor except Lemon**
2 **cups milk**
2 **cups thawed COOL WHIP® Non-Dairy Whipped Topping**

Combine pudding mix and milk in medium saucepan; blend well. Cook and stir over medium heat until mixture comes to a full boil. Pour into bowl; cover surface of pudding with plastic wrap. Chill.

Spoon ⅓ cup of the whipped topping into each of 6 dessert glasses. Using the back of a spoon, make a depression in the center and spread topping up the sides of each glass. Spoon pudding mixture into glasses. Chill.

QUICK COFFEE FLUFF

Makes 8 or 9 servings

1 **tablespoon MAXWELL HOUSE® or YUBAN®
    Instant Coffee**
2¼ **cups cold milk**
1 **envelope DREAM WHIP® Whipped Topping Mix**
1 **package (6-serving size) JELL-O® Vanilla Flavor Instant
    Pudding and Pie Filling**
½ **teaspoon cinnamon (optional)**
½ **cup chopped nuts (optional)**

Dissolve coffee in milk in bowl. Add whipped topping mix, pudding mix and cinnamon. With electric mixer at low speed, beat until well blended, about 1 minute. Gradually increase beating speed and beat until mixture forms soft peaks, 3 to 6 minutes. Fold in nuts. Spoon into individual dessert glasses. Chill. Garnish with additional whipped topping and pecan halves.

*Clockwise from top: Pudding Tart-in-a-Dish (see page 56),
Quick Coffee Fluff, Pudding in a Cloud*

■ ■ ■

■ ■ ■

PUDDING TART-IN-A-DISH

Makes about 2½ cups or 4 servings

- 1 package (4-serving size) JELL-O® Pudding and Pie Filling, any flavor except Lemon
- 2 cups milk
- ½ cup graham cracker crumbs or cookie crumbs
- 2 to 3 teaspoons butter or margarine, melted

Combine pudding mix and milk in medium saucepan; blend well. Cook and stir over medium heat until mixture comes to a full boil. Cool 5 minutes, stirring twice.

Combine crumbs and butter; mix well. Press mixture on bottom and sides of individual dessert glasses. Spoon pudding into crumb-lined glasses. Chill. Garnish with prepared whipped topping and additional crumbs, if desired.

PUDDING POKE CAKE

Makes one 13×9-inch cake

- 1 package (2-layer size) yellow cake mix or pudding-included cake mix*
  Ingredients for cake mix (see package)
- 2 packages (4-serving size) JELL-O® Chocolate Flavor Instant Pudding and Pie Filling*
- 1 cup confectioners sugar
- 4 cups cold milk

Prepare and bake cake mix as directed on package for 13×9-inch cake. Remove from oven. Poke holes at once down through cake to pan with round handle of wooden spoon. (Or poke holes with plastic drinking straw, using turning motion to make large holes.) Holes should be at 1-inch intervals.

Only after the holes are made, combine pudding mix with sugar in large bowl. Gradually stir in milk. Beat with electric mixer at low speed for not more than 1 minute. Do not overbeat. Quickly, before pudding thickens, pour about half of the thin pudding evenly over warm cake and into holes.

CONTINUED

■ ■ ■

(This will make stripes in cake.) Allow remaining pudding to thicken slightly; then spoon over the top, swirling it to "frost" the cake. Chill at least 1 hour. Store cake in refrigerator.

Peanut Butter Poke Cake: Prepare Pudding Poke Cake as directed, using chocolate flavor instant pudding and pie filling. Add ½ cup peanut butter to pudding mix and confectioners sugar with ½ cup of the milk; blend well before adding remaining milk and beating.

*Additional Flavor Combinations
Use yellow cake mix with butterscotch or pistachio flavor pudding mix.

Use chocolate cake mix with chocolate, vanilla, coconut cream, banana cream or pistachio flavor pudding mix.

Use lemon cake mix with lemon flavor pudding mix.

Use white cake mix with butterscotch, chocolate, pistachio or vanilla pudding mix.

■ ■ ■

■ ■ ■

LAYERED FRUIT SALAD

Makes about 5½ cups or 10 servings

  2 **packages (4-serving size) JELL-O® Brand Orange or Wild Strawberry Flavor Gelatin**
1½ **cups boiling water**
  1 **cup cold water**
    Ice cubes
  2 **tablespoons lemon juice**
  2 **cups fresh fruit (banana slices, orange sections and halved seedless grapes)**
  1 **package (3 ounces) cream cheese, softened**
 ⅛ **teaspoon cinnamon**

Completely dissolve gelatin in boiling water. Combine cold water and ice cubes to make 2½ cups. Add to gelatin with lemon juice, stirring until slightly thickened. Remove any unmelted ice. Measure 1 cup of the gelatin; set aside. Stir fruit into remaining gelatin; pour into serving bowl. Place measured gelatin, cheese and cinnamon in blender. Cover and blend until smooth. Spoon carefully over gelatin mixture in bowl. Chill until set, about 2 hours.

■ ■ ■

FRUITED TILT

Makes 6 to 8 servings

1 package (4-serving size) JELL-O® Brand Gelatin, any
   flavor
¾ cup boiling water
½ cup cold water
   Ice cubes
1 cup sliced or diced fresh fruit*
1 cup thawed COOL WHIP® Non-Dairy Whipped Topping

Dissolve gelatin in boiling water. Combine cold water and ice cubes to make 1¼ cups. Add to gelatin, stirring until slightly thickened. Remove any unmelted ice. Fold in fruit. Spoon half of the fruited gelatin into individual parfait glasses. Tilt glasses in refrigerator by catching bases between bars of rack and leaning tops against wall; chill until set. Spoon whipped topping into glasses; top with remaining fruited gelatin. Stand glasses upright. Chill about 30 minutes.

*Do not use fresh pineapple, kiwifruit, mango, papaya or figs.

FLUFFY RASPBERRY PARFAIT

Makes about 2½ cups or 5 servings

1½ cups cold milk
1 envelope DREAM WHIP® Whipped Topping Mix
¼ teaspoon almond extract
1 package (4-serving size) JELL-O® Vanilla Flavor Instant
   Pudding and Pie Filling
⅓ cup raspberry jam

Combine ½ cup of the cold milk and the whipped topping mix in bowl. With electric mixer at low speed, beat until blended. Beat at high speed for about 4 minutes or until topping thickens and forms peaks, scraping bowl often. Add remaining milk, the extract and pudding mix. Blend; then beat at high speed for 2 minutes. Spoon half of the pudding mixture into individual dessert dishes. Add about 1 tablespoon jam to each glass. Top with remaining pudding mixture. Chill 30 minutes. Garnish with additional jam, if desired.

■ ■ ■

■ ■ ■

MANDARIN PARFAITS

Makes 6 servings

1 **cup cold milk**
1 **cup (½ pint) sour cream**
¼ **teaspoon almond extract**
1 **package (4-serving size) JELL-O® Vanilla or French Vanilla Flavor Instant Pudding and Pie Filling**
1 **can (11 ounces) mandarin orange sections, drained**

Combine milk, sour cream and almond extract in bowl. Add pudding mix. With electric mixer at low speed, beat until well blended, 1 to 2 minutes. Layer pudding and orange sections in individual parfait glasses. Chill about 1 hour. Garnish with whipped topping, if desired.

CREAMY FRUIT PUDDING

Makes about 4 cups or 8 servings

1 **can (16 to 17 ounces) sliced peaches, fruit cocktail, apricot halves or peach halves**
1 **cup cold milk**
1 **package (4-serving size) JELL-O® Vanilla or Lemon Flavor Instant Pudding and Pie Filling**
1 **envelope DREAM WHIP® Whipped Topping Mix**

Drain peaches, reserving syrup. Add cold water to syrup to make 1 cup; set aside. Dice peaches, reserving 2 tablespoons for garnish, if desired.

Pour cold milk into bowl. Add pudding mix and whipped topping mix. With electric mixer at low speed, beat until thoroughly blended. Add measured liquid and beat at medium speed for 3 minutes. Fold peaches into pudding mixture; spoon into individual dessert dishes. Garnish with reserved diced peaches. Chill about 1 hour.

■ ■ ■

Mandarin Parfaits

■ ■ ■

LIGHT AND FRUITY PIE

Makes one 9-inch pie

  1 package (4-serving size) JELL-O® Brand Gelatin, any
      flavor
  ⅔ cup boiling water
  ½ cup cold water
      Ice cubes
 3½ cups (8 ounces) COOL WHIP® Non-Dairy Whipped
      Topping, thawed
  1 cup diced peeled fresh peaches, apricots or pears*
  1 prepared 9-inch graham cracker crumb crust, cooled

Completely dissolve gelatin in boiling water. Combine cold water and ice cubes to make 1¼ cups. Add to gelatin, stirring until slightly thickened. Remove any unmelted ice. Using wire whisk, blend in whipped topping. Fold in fruit. Chill until mixture mounds. Spoon into pie crust. Chill about 2 hours. Garnish with additional fruit, if desired.

*Substitutions:
Use 1 cup fresh raspberries or blueberries or halved pitted dark sweet cherries.

Use 1 cup diced orange sections, banana or strawberries.

FAST AND FABULOUS FRUIT

Makes 3 cups or 6 servings

  1 package (4-serving size) JELL-O® Instant Pudding and
      Pie Filling, any flavor
  1 can (20 ounces) crushed pineapple in juice*
  1 cup thawed COOL WHIP® Non-Dairy Whipped Topping**

Combine pudding mix and fruit with juice in bowl. With electric mixer at low speed, beat until well blended, 1 to 2 minutes. Blend in whipped topping. Spoon into individual dessert dishes. Garnish as desired.

*Substitution: Use 1 can (16 ounces) sliced peaches, or 1 can (17 ounces) fruit cocktail, pitted dark sweet cherries or apricot halves, diced.

**Substitution: Use 1 cup sour cream, whipped cream cheese, cottage cheese or plain yogurt.

■ ■ ▣

···

FROZEN PEANUT BUTTER PIE

Makes one 9-inch pie

3½ cups (8 ounces) COOL WHIP® Non-Dairy Whipped
   Topping, thawed
 1 prepared 9-inch graham cracker crumb crust, cooled
 ⅓ cup strawberry jam
 1 cup cold milk
 ½ cup chunky peanut butter
 1 package (4-serving size) JELL-O® Vanilla Flavor Instant
   Pudding and Pie Filling

Spread 1 cup of the whipped topping in bottom of pie crust; freeze for about 10 minutes. Carefully spoon jam over whipped topping.

Gradually add milk to peanut butter in bowl, blending until smooth. Add pie filling mix. With electric mixer at low speed, beat until well blended, 1 to 2 minutes. Fold in remaining whipped topping. Spoon over jam in pie crust. Freeze until firm, about 4 hours. Garnish with additional whipped topping and chopped nuts, if desired.

LAYERED PUDDING

Makes about 2½ cups or 4 servings

1½ cups cold milk

  1 package (4-serving size) JELL-O® Instant Pudding and
      Pie Filling, any flavor

  1 cup thawed COOL WHIP® Non-Dairy Whipped Topping

Pour cold milk into bowl. Add pudding mix. With electric mixer at low speed, beat for 1 minute. Spoon ¼ cup of the pudding into each of 4 dessert glasses. Fold whipped topping into remaining pudding. Spoon over plain pudding in glasses. Garnish with additional whipped topping and chocolate curls, if desired.

Three Layer Pudding: Prepare Layered Pudding as directed, increasing whipped topping to 1¾ cups. Fold 1 cup of the whipped topping into ½ cup of the pudding; layer with remaining plain pudding and remaining whipped topping in 6 parfait glasses. Makes about 3½ cups or 6 servings.

■ ■ ■

■ ■ ■

CHERRY CHEESE MOLD

Makes 4 cups or 8 servings

1 can (8 ounces) dark sweet pitted cherries
1 package (4-serving size) JELL-O® Brand Cherry Flavor
   Gelatin
1½ cups crushed ice
2 packages (3 ounces each) cream cheese, softened and
   cut up

Drain cherries, reserving syrup. Add water to syrup to make ¾ cup. Pour into small saucepan. Bring to a boil over high heat. Pour boiling liquid into blender. Add gelatin. Cover and blend at low speed until gelatin is completely dissolved, about 30 seconds. Add crushed ice and cream cheese. Blend at high speed for 1 minute. Pour into 4-cup mold or bowl or individual dessert dishes. Drop cherries into gelatin mixture, one at a time. Chill until firm, about 1 hour. Unmold.

ORANGE COCONUT CREAM PUDDING

Makes 4 servings

1 package (4-serving size) JELL-O® Coconut Cream,
   Vanilla, Chocolate or Chocolate Fudge Flavor Pudding
   and Pie Filling
1½ cups milk
½ cup orange juice
½ teaspoon grated orange rind

Microwave: Combine pudding mix and milk in 1½-quart microwave-safe bowl; blend well. Cook at HIGH 3 minutes. Stir well and cook 2 minutes longer; then stir again and cook 1 minute or until mixture comes to a boil. Stir in orange juice and rind. Spoon into individual dessert dishes. Chill.

*Ovens vary. Cooking time is approximate.

■ ■ ■

■ ■ ■

SOUR CREAM PUDDING

Makes about 2 cups or 4 servings

1 package (4-serving size) JELL-O® Pudding and Pie Filling,
   any flavor except lemon
3 tablespoons sugar
1 cup water
1 cup (½ pint) sour cream

Range Top: Combine pudding mix, sugar and water in medium saucepan; blend well. Cook and stir over medium heat until mixture comes to a full boil. Cool 5 minutes, stirring twice. Stir in sour cream, blending well. Pour into bowl or dessert glasses. Chill. Garnish with whipped topping, and sprinkle with nutmeg or chocolate curls, if desired.

Microwave: * Combine pudding mix, sugar and water in 1½-quart microwave-safe bowl; blend well. Cook at HIGH 3 minutes. Stir well and cook 2 minutes longer; then stir again and cook 1 minute or until mixture comes to a boil. Cool 5 minutes, stirring twice. Stir in sour cream, blending well. Pour into bowl or dessert glasses. Chill. Garnish with whipped topping, and sprinkle with nutmeg or chocolate curls, if desired.

*Ovens vary. Cooking time is approximate.

RIPPLE DESSERT

Makes about 2½ cups or 5 servings

2 cups cold milk
1 package (4-serving size) JELL-O® Vanilla Flavor Instant
   Pudding and Pie Filling
1 cup thawed COOL WHIP® Non-Dairy Whipped Topping
3 tablespoons chocolate syrup*

Pour cold milk into bowl. Add pudding mix. With electric mixer at low speed, beat until well blended, 1 to 2 minutes. Fold in whipped topping. Layer pudding mixture and syrup in individual parfait glasses. Chill. Garnish with additional whipped topping and syrup, if desired.

*Substitution: Use ¼ cup raspberry or strawberry preserves thinned with ½ teaspoon water.

■ ■ ■

■ ■ ■

FRUIT WHIP

Makes 4½ cups or 6 servings

¾ cup boiling water

1 package (4-serving size) JELL-O® Brand Gelatin, any flavor

½ cup cold water or fruit juice
   Ice cubes

1 cup fresh or canned fruit (optional)

Pour boiling water into blender. Add gelatin. Cover and blend at low speed until gelatin is completely dissolved, about 30 seconds. Combine cold water and ice cubes to make 1¼ cups. Add to gelatin and stir until ice is partially melted; then blend at high speed for 30 seconds. Pour into dessert glasses or serving bowl. Spoon in fruit. Chill until firm, 20 to 30 minutes. Dessert layers as it chills.

■ ■ ■

PINEAPPLE-COCONUT PIE

Makes one 9-inch pie

1 package (4-serving size) JELL-O® Brand Orange Flavor
  Gelatin
⅔ cup boiling water
¼ cup rum or 1½ teaspoons rum extract
½ cup cold water
  Ice cubes
3½ cups (8 ounces) COOL WHIP® Non-Dairy Whipped
  Topping, thawed
1 can (8¼ ounces) crushed pineapple, drained
½ cup BAKER'S® ANGEL FLAKE® Coconut
1 prepared 9-inch graham cracker crumb crust, cooled

Completely dissolve gelatin in boiling water. Stir in rum. Combine cold water and ice cubes to make 1¼ cups. Add to gelatin, stirring until slightly thickened. Remove any unmelted ice. Using wire whisk, blend in whipped topping; then whip until smooth. Fold in pineapple and coconut. Chill until mixture mounds. Spoon into pie crust. Chill about 2 hours. Garnish with pineapple chunks and additional coconut, if desired.

PUDDING PEACH SHORTCAKE

Makes 4 servings

1 cup cold milk
1 cup (½ pint) sour cream
⅛ teaspoon almond extract
1 package (4-serving size) JELL-O® Vanilla Flavor Instant
  Pudding and Pie Filling
8 thin slices pound cake
1½ cups sliced peeled peaches

Combine cold milk, sour cream and almond extract in bowl. Add pudding mix. With electric mixer at low speed, beat until well blended, 1 to 2 minutes. Let stand 5 minutes. Place a slice of pound cake in each of 4 dessert dishes. Spoon ¼ cup of the pudding onto each slice. Top with half of the peaches. Repeat layers with remaining ingredients. Garnish with whipped topping, if desired.

■ ■ ■

■ ■ ■

GLAZED PEACH CREME

Makes 5 cups or 10 servings

2 packages (4-serving size) or 1 package (8-serving size)
   JELL-O® Brand Peach, Orange, Raspberry or Black
   Cherry Flavor Gelatin
2 cups boiling water
¾ cup cold water
2 cups (1 pint) vanilla ice cream
1 can (8¾ ounces) sliced peaches, drained, or 1 sliced
   peeled fresh peach

Completely dissolve gelatin in boiling water. Measure 1 cup of the gelatin; add cold water. Chill until slightly thickened.

Add ice cream to remaining gelatin; stir until melted and smooth. Pour ice cream mixture into serving bowl or individual dessert glasses. Chill until set but not firm. Arrange peach slices on ice cream layer in bowl. Spoon clear gelatin over peaches. Chill until set, about 4 hours.

SELF-LAYERING DESSERT

Makes 3 cups or 6 servings

¾ cup boiling water
1 package (4-serving size) JELL-O® Brand Gelatin, any
   flavor
½ cup cold water
   Ice cubes
½ cup thawed COOL WHIP® Non-Dairy Whipped Topping

Pour boiling water into blender. Add gelatin. Cover and blend at low speed until gelatin is completely dissolved, about 30 seconds. Combine cold water and ice cubes to make 1¼ cups. Add to gelatin and stir until ice is partially melted. Then add whipped topping; blend at high speed for 30 seconds. Pour into dessert glasses. Chill about 30 minutes. Dessert layers as it chills. Garnish as desired.

■ ■ ■

■ ■ ■

FRUITED CHIFFON SQUARES

Makes about 4½ cups or 9 servings

2 packages (4-serving size) or 1 package (8-serving size)
   JELL-O® Brand Gelatin, any flavor
1½ cups boiling water
 1 cup cold water
   Ice cubes
1¾ cups thawed COOL WHIP® Non-Dairy Whipped Topping
 1 can (8 to 8½ ounces) fruit, drained, or 1 cup sliced or
   diced fresh fruit*

Completely dissolve gelatin in boiling water. Combine cold water and ice cubes to make 2½ cups. Add to gelatin, stirring until slightly thickened. Remove any unmelted ice. Measure 1 cup of the gelatin; fold into whipped topping. Pour into 8-inch square pan. Chill about 10 minutes. Add fruit to remaining gelatin; gently spoon over creamy layer in pan. Chill until firm, about 3 hours. Cut into squares. Garnish as desired.

*Do not use fresh pineapple, kiwifruit, mango, papaya or figs.

FOAMY PEACH DESSERT

Makes 3½ cups or 6 or 7 servings

1 can (8¾ ounces) sliced peaches in light syrup
1 package (4-serving size) JELL-O® Brand Gelatin, any
   flavor
1½ cups ice cubes

Drain peaches, reserving syrup. Add water to syrup to make ¾ cup; pour into small saucepan. Bring to a boil over high heat. Pour boiling liquid into blender. Add gelatin. Cover and blend at high speed until gelatin is completely dissolved, about 1 minute. Add ice cubes and stir until ice is partially melted. Add peaches. Blend at high speed for 2 minutes or until ice is melted and mixture is smooth. Pour into serving bowl or individual dessert dishes. Chill until set, about 2 hours.

■ ■ ■

UNDER-THE-SEA SALAD

Makes about 3½ cups or 6 servings

- 1 can (16 ounces) pear halves in syrup
- 1 package (4-serving size) JELL-O® Brand Lime Flavor Gelatin
- ¼ teaspoon salt (optional)
- 1 cup boiling water
- 1 tablespoon lemon juice
- 2 packages (3 ounces each) cream cheese, softened
- ⅛ teaspoon cinnamon (optional)

Drain pears, reserving ¾ cup of the syrup. Dice pears; set aside. Dissolve gelatin and salt in boiling water. Add reserved syrup and lemon juice. Measure 1¼ cups of the gelatin; pour into 8×4-inch loaf pan or 4-cup mold. Chill until set but not firm, about 1 hour.

Very slowly blend remaining gelatin into cream cheese, beating until smooth. Add cinnamon and pears; spoon over clear gelatin in pan. Chill until firm, about 4 hours. Unmold. Garnish with additional pears and maraschino cherry, if desired.

■ ■ ■

CUP OF TRIFLE

Makes about 3½ cups or 6 servings

1½ cups ½-inch pound cake cubes

  2 tablespoons orange juice

  3 tablespoons raspberry preserves

  1 tablespoon water

1½ cups cold milk

  1 package (4-serving size) JELL-O® French Vanilla or
     Vanilla Instant Pudding and Pie Filling*

1¾ cups thawed COOL WHIP® Non-Dairy Whipped Topping

  1 tablespoon sherry wine (optional)*   CONTINUED

■ ■ ■

■ ■ ■

Arrange cake cubes in individual dessert glasses; sprinkle with orange juice. Combine raspberry preserves with water. Spoon over cake cubes.

Pour cold milk into bowl. Add pudding mix. With electric mixer at low speed, beat until well blended, 1 to 2 minutes. Blend in 1 cup of the whipped topping and the sherry. Spoon over preserves in glasses. Chill. Garnish with remaining whipped topping, stemmed maraschino cherries and toasted slivered almonds, if desired.

*Substitution: Use chocolate flavor instant pudding and pie filling and 2 tablespoons almond liqueur.

APRICOT CHIFFON

Makes about 4 cups or 8 servings

- 1 can (8½ ounces) apricot halves in light syrup
- ¾ cup boiling water
- 1 package (4-serving size) JELL-O® Brand Apricot Flavor Gelatin
- 1 teaspoon grated lemon rind (optional)
- 1 tablespoon lemon juice
  Ice cubes
- 1¾ cups thawed COOL WHIP® Non-Dairy Whipped Topping

Drain apricots, reserving syrup. Combine syrup and water to make ½ cup; set aside. Dice apricots and divide among individual parfait glasses. Pour boiling water into blender. Add gelatin, lemon rind and lemon juice. Cover and blend at low speed until gelatin is completely dissolved, about 30 seconds. Combine measured liquid and ice cubes to make 1¼ cups. Add to gelatin and stir until ice is partially melted. Then add whipped topping; blend at high speed 30 seconds. Pour over fruit in glasses. Chill until set, about 30 minutes. Garnish with additional whipped topping and fruit, if desired.

Orange-Pineapple Chiffon: Prepare Apricot Chiffon as directed, substituting 1 can (8¼ ounces) crushed pineapple in juice and orange-pineapple flavor gelatin for the apricots and apricot flavor gelatin.

Peach Chiffon: Prepare Apricot Chiffon as directed, substituting 1 can (8¼ to 8¾ ounces) sliced peaches and peach flavor gelatin for the apricots and apricot flavor gelatin.

■ ■ ■

SPECIAL OCCASIONS

Impress your guests with one of these dazzling creations. What better way to celebrate with family and friends.

Cherry-Topped Icebox Cake

■ ■ ■

CHERRY-TOPPED ICEBOX CAKE

Makes 12 servings

20 whole graham crackers
 2 cups cold milk
 1 package (6-serving size) JELL-O® Vanilla or Chocolate
   Flavor Instant Pudding and Pie Filling
1¾ cups thawed COOL WHIP® Non-Dairy Whipped Topping
 2 cans (21 ounces each) cherry pie filling

Line 13×9-inch pan with some of the graham crackers, breaking crackers, if necessary. Pour cold milk into bowl. Add pudding mix. With electric mixer at low speed, beat until well blended, 1 to 2 minutes. Let stand 5 minutes; then blend in whipped topping. Spread half of the pudding mixture over crackers. Add another layer of crackers. Top with remaining pudding mixture and remaining crackers. Spread cherry pie filling over crackers. Chill about 3 hours.

Chocolate-Frosted Icebox Cake: Prepare Cherry-Topped Icebox Cake as directed, substituting ¾ cup ready-to-spread chocolate fudge frosting for the cherry pie filling. Carefully spread frosting over graham crackers.

CREME BRULÉE

Makes 4½ cups or 8 to 10 servings

1 package (6-serving size) JELL-O® Vanilla Flavor Pudding
   and Pie Filling
1 quart light cream or half and half
2 eggs, slightly beaten
1 teaspoon vanilla
¼ cup packed brown sugar, sieved

Combine pudding mix and cream in medium saucepan; blend well. Cook and stir over medium heat until mixture comes to a full boil. Remove from heat. Stir small amount of hot mixture into eggs, mixing well. Return egg mixture to remaining hot mixture, stirring constantly. Cook over low heat for 1 minute, stirring constantly. Add vanilla and pour into shallow 1½-quart baking dish. Chill at least 3 hours. Evenly sprinkle brown sugar over top of pudding. Broil until sugar melts, about 1½ minutes. Serve warm or chill. Serve over fruit or cake, if desired.

■ ■ ■

■ ■ ■

MOLDED CHEESE

Makes 5½ cups or 11 servings

2 packages (4-serving size) or 1 package (8-serving size)
    JELL-O® Brand Orange or Lemon Flavor Gelatin
1½ cups boiling water
 ½ pound (2½ cups) finely grated sharp Cheddar cheese
  1 package (8 ounces) cream cheese, softened
  1 cup (½ pint) sour cream
 ½ cup chopped scallions
 ¼ cup chopped parsley
  3 tablespoons prepared horseradish
  1 tablespoon Worcestershire sauce

Dissolve gelatin in boiling water. Combine remaining ingredients in large bowl; with electric mixer at medium speed, beat until well blended. Gradually blend into gelatin. Pour into 6-cup mold. Chill until firm, about 3 hours. Unmold. Garnish with fresh fruit or vegetables, if desired. Serve as an appetizer with assorted crackers.

PUDDING PECAN PIE

Makes one 8-inch pie

1 package (4-serving size) JELL-O® Vanilla or
    Butterscotch Flavor Instant Pudding and Pie Filling*
1 cup light or dark corn syrup
¾ cup evaporated milk
1 egg, slightly beaten
1 cup chopped pecans*
1 unbaked 8-inch pie shell

Combine pie filling mix with corn syrup in medium bowl. With electric mixer at low speed, blend. Gradually add evaporated milk and egg; blend well. Stir in nuts; pour into pie shell. Bake in preheated 375° oven until top is firm and just begins to crack, 45 to 50 minutes. Cool on wire rack at least 3 hours before serving. Garnish with whipped topping and additional pecans, if desired.

*Substitution: Use butter pecan flavor instant pudding and pie filling, reducing pecans to ½ cup.

■ ■ ■

BUFFET LEMON CHEESECAKE

Makes 9 to 12 servings

1¼ cups graham cracker crumbs

3 tablespoons sugar

⅓ cup butter or margarine, melted

2 packages (8 ounces each) cream cheese, softened

4 cups cold milk

2 packages (4-serving size) JELL-O® Lemon Flavor Instant Pudding and Pie Filling

Combine crumbs, sugar and butter; mix well. Press firmly on bottom and side of 9- or 10-inch springform pan. Bake in preheated 350° oven for about 8 minutes, or until lightly browned. Cool on wire rack.

Place cream cheese in large bowl. With electric mixer at medium speed, beat until smooth. Gradually add 1 cup of the milk, blending until mixture is very smooth. Add remaining milk and the pudding mix. Beat at low speed just until well blended, about 1 minute. Pour carefully into crumb-lined pan. Chill until firm, about 3 hours. Garnish with lemon slice and mint, if desired.

■ ■ ■

Banana and Sour Cream Mold

Makes about 5 cups or 10 servings

 2 packages (4-serving size) JELL-O® Brand Lime or Lemon
   Flavor Gelatin
 2 cups boiling water
1¼ cups cold water
 1 small banana, sliced
 ½ cup sour cream
 ¼ cup diced celery
 ¼ cup chopped walnuts or pecans

CONTINUED

• • •

■ ■ ■

Dissolve 1 package of the gelatin in 1 cup of the boiling water. Add ¾ cup of the cold water and chill until thickened. Stir in banana and spoon into 6-cup ring mold. Chill until set but not firm, about 15 minutes.

Meanwhile, dissolve remaining gelatin in remaining boiling water. Add remaining cold water and chill until slightly thickened. Blend in sour cream. Stir in celery and nuts. Spoon over fruited gelatin in mold. Chill until firm, about 4 hours. Unmold. Garnish with lettuce and walnut halves, if desired.

STRAWBERRY-PEACH UPSIDE DOWN CAKE

Makes one 13×9-inch cake

> 1 can (29 ounces) sliced peaches, drained, or 2 cups sliced peeled fresh peaches
> 1 package (4-serving size) JELL-O® Brand Strawberry Flavor Gelatin
> 1 package (4-serving size) JELL-O® Brand Peach Flavor Gelatin
> 1 teaspoon cinnamon (optional)
> ⅓ cup butter or margarine
> 1 package (2-layer size) yellow cake mix or pudding-included cake mix
> Ingredients for cake mix (see package)

Arrange peaches in buttered 13×9-inch pan. Combine strawberry and peach flavor gelatins and cinnamon in small bowl. Sprinkle about ¾ of the mixture evenly over peaches; dot with butter.

Prepare cake mix according to package directions. Pour ¾ of the batter into pan. Stir remaining gelatin mixture into remaining cake batter; blend well and pour over batter in pan. Swirl spatula through batter to marble. Bake in preheated 350° oven for 45 minutes, or until cake tester inserted in center of cake comes out clean and cake begins to pull away from sides of pan. Cool in pan on wire rack 5 minutes. Invert onto serving platter and cool. Garnish with whipped topping, if desired.

■ ■ ■

Peach Melba Parfait (see page 82),
Topaz Parfait, Banana-Rum Parfait

■ ■ ■

TOPAZ PARFAIT

Makes 4 to 6 servings

- 1 cup brewed MAXWELL HOUSE® or YUBAN® Coffee
- 1 package (4-serving size) JELL-O® Brand Lemon Flavor Gelatin
- 1/3 cup granulated sugar
- 1/2 cup cold water
- 1/4 cup brandy or dark rum
- 2 tablespoons brown sugar
- 1 tablespoon brandy or dark rum
- 1¾ cups thawed COOL WHIP® Non-Dairy Whipped Topping

Bring coffee to a boil. Add gelatin and granulated sugar; stir until dissolved. Add cold water and the 1/4 cup brandy. Pour into 8-inch square pan. Chill until firm, about 4 hours.

Cut gelatin into cubes or flake with fork. Fold brown sugar and the 1 tablespoon brandy into whipped topping. Layer gelatin cubes and topping in parfait glasses or top cubes in dessert glasses with topping.

BANANA-RUM PARFAIT

Makes 2¾ cups or 5 servings

- 1 package (4-serving size) JELL-O® Brand Lemon, Orange or Strawberry Flavor Gelatin
- 1 cup boiling water
- 1/4 cup cold water
  - Ice cubes
- 1 medium banana, sliced
- 1 cup (1/2 pint) vanilla ice cream
- 1 tablespoon light rum or 1/4 teaspoon rum extract

Completely dissolve gelatin in boiling water. Measure 1/2 cup of the gelatin. Combine cold water and ice cubes to make 3/4 cup. Add to measured gelatin, stirring until slightly thickened. Remove any unmelted ice. Stir in banana and spoon into individual parfait glasses. Blend ice cream and rum into remaining gelatin. Spoon over fruited gelatin in glasses. Chill until set, about 30 minutes. Garnish as desired.

■ ■ ■

■ ■ ■

PEACH MELBA PARFAIT

Makes about 2½ cups or 5 servings

1 package (3 ounces) cream cheese, softened
1 tablespoon sugar
1 tablespoon milk
1 package (4-serving size) JELL-O® Brand Peach Flavor
  Gelatin
¾ cup boiling water
½ cup cold water
  Ice cubes
1 cup diced peeled peaches or 1 can (8¾ ounces) peaches,
  drained and diced
¼ cup raspberry jam or preserves

Combine cream cheese, sugar and milk in bowl. With electric mixer at medium speed, blend well; set aside. Completely dissolve gelatin in boiling water. Combine cold water and ice cubes to make 1¼ cups. Add to gelatin, stirring until slightly thickened. Remove any unmelted ice. Fold in peaches.

Spoon half of the fruited gelatin into parfait or wine glasses. Carefully spoon about 1 tablespoon of the cheese mixture over fruited gelatin in each glass; add scant tablespoon of the jam. Spoon remaining fruited gelatin over jam in glasses. Chill until set, about 2 hours. Garnish with whipped topping and peach slices, if desired.

CRANBERRY-LEMON PIE

Makes one 9-inch pie

1 package (4-serving size) JELL-O® Brand Lemon Flavor
  Gelatin
¾ cup boiling water
1 can (16 ounces) whole berry cranberry sauce
1¾ cups thawed COOL WHIP® Non-Dairy Whipped Topping
1 baked 9-inch pie shell, cooled

Dissolve gelatin in boiling water. Add cranberry sauce; mix well. Chill until slightly thickened. Fold in whipped topping. Spoon into pie shell. Chill until set, about 2 hours. Garnish with additional whipped topping, lemon slices or fresh cranberries, if desired.

■ ■ ■

CREAMY MELON LAYERED SALAD

Makes 3 cups or 6 servings

- 1 package (4-serving size) JELL-O® Brand Lemon or Lime Flavor Gelatin
- 1 cup boiling water
- ¾ cup cold water
- 1 teaspoon lemon juice
- ½ to 1 cup cantaloupe or honeydew melon balls or diced melon (about 1 small)
- ¼ cup sliced celery
- ¼ cup slivered almonds (optional)
- 1 package (3 ounces) cream cheese, softened
- ⅓ cup mayonnaise

Dissolve gelatin in boiling water. Add cold water and lemon juice. Chill until slightly thickened. Measure 1¼ cups of the gelatin; fold in melon balls, celery and nuts. Pour into 4-cup ring mold or individual molds. Chill until set but not firm.

Blend cream cheese and mayonnaise until smooth. Gradually blend in remaining gelatin. Pour over clear gelatin in mold. Chill until firm, about 3 hours. Unmold. Garnish with additional melon balls and crisp greens, if desired.

PINEAPPLE RASPBERRY TORTE

Makes 12 servings

- 1 package (4-serving size) JELL-O® Brand Raspberry Flavor Gelatin
- 1¼ cups boiling water
- 1 can (20 ounces) crushed pineapple
- 2 baked 9-inch white cake layers, cooled
- 1¾ cups thawed COOL WHIP® Non-Dairy Whipped Topping

Dissolve gelatin in boiling water. Stir in undrained pineapple and chill until very thick. Spread half of the gelatin mixture on top of each cake layer and chill until firm, about 3 hours. Spread half of the whipped topping over the gelatin on 1 layer. Top with remaining layer, gelatin-side up, and remaining whipped topping. Chill.

CHIFFON PARTY DESSERT

Makes 5 cups or 10 servings

2 packages (4-serving size) or 1 package (8-serving size)
   JELL-O® Brand Black Raspberry, Orange or Black
   Cherry Flavor Gelatin
2 cups boiling water
1 quart vanilla ice cream
12 ladyfingers, split

CONTINUED

■ ■ ■

Completely dissolve gelatin in boiling water. Add ice cream by spoonfuls, stirring until completely melted. Chill until thickened.

Meanwhile, trim off about 1 inch of the ladyfingers and place cut ends down around side of 8-inch springform pan. Spoon gelatin mixture into pan. Chill until firm, about 3 hours. Remove side of pan. Garnish with whipped topping, fresh fruit and mint leaves, if desired.

FRESH FRUIT MOUSSE

Makes 6 cups or 12 servings

    1 cup boiling water
    1 package (4-serving size) JELL-O® Brand Lemon or
       Strawberry Flavor Gelatin*
   ¾ cup sugar
    1 pint strawberries, hulled*
    2 egg whites**
 1¾ cups thawed COOL WHIP® Non-Dairy Whipped Topping

Pour boiling water into blender. Add gelatin and ½ cup of the sugar. Cover and blend at low speed until completely dissolved, about 30 seconds. Blend in strawberries, a few at a time, at high speed until pureed. Chill until slightly thickened, about 2 hours.

With electric mixer at medium speed, beat egg whites until foamy. Gradually add remaining sugar, beating thoroughly after each addition. Continue beating at high speed until mixture forms stiff shiny peaks. Fold in whipped topping; then fold in thickened fruit mixture. Spoon into dessert glasses. Garnish with additional whipped topping, if desired.

*Additional Flavor Combinations
Use peach flavor gelatin with 2 medium peeled and quartered peaches.

Use lemon flavor gelatin with 3 peeled and quartered plums.

Use lime flavor gelatin with 2 medium peeled, cored and quartered pears.

**Use only clean eggs with no cracks in shells.

■ ■ ■

■ ■ ■

GLAZED FRUIT PIE

Makes one 9-inch pie

1½ cups cold milk or half and half
1 package (4-serving size) JELL-O® Vanilla Flavor Instant
    Pudding and Pie Filling
1 baked 9-inch pie shell or prepared graham cracker crumb
    crust, cooled
1 package (4-serving size) JELL-O® Brand Peach or Orange
    Flavor Gelatin, or any red flavor
1 cup boiling water
½ cup cold water
2 cups (about) fresh or drained canned fruit*

Pour cold milk into bowl. Add pie filling mix. With electric mixer at low speed, beat 1 minute. Pour into pie shell. Chill 1 hour.

Dissolve gelatin in boiling water. Add cold water. Chill until thickened. Pour about ½ cup of the gelatin over pie filling in pie shell. Arrange fruit on gelatin and spoon remaining gelatin over fruit. Chill about 2 hours.

*Do not use fresh pineapple, kiwifruit, mango, papaya or figs.

FRENCH CHERRY PIE

Makes one 8-inch pie

1 cup cold milk
1 cup (½ pint) sour cream
¼ teaspoon almond extract
1 package (4-serving size) JELL-O® Vanilla or French
    Vanilla Flavor Instant Pudding and Pie Filling
1 prepared 8-inch graham cracker crumb crust or baked
    pie shell, cooled
1 can (21 ounces) cherry pie filling

Combine cold milk, sour cream and almond extract in bowl. Add pie filling mix. With electric mixer at low speed, beat until blended, about 1 minute. Pour immediately into pie crust. Chill about 2 hours. Spoon cherry pie filling over pie.

■ ■ ■

Glazed Fruit Pie

■ ■ ■

STRAWBERRY SQUARES

Makes 8 cups or 15 servings

1½ cups all-purpose flour
½ cup finely chopped pecans
½ cup butter or margarine, melted
2 packages (4-serving size) or 1 package (8-serving size)
    JELL-O® Brand Strawberry Flavor Gelatin
2 packages (4-serving size) JELL-O® Vanilla Flavor
    Pudding and Pie Filling
2½ cups water
3 pints strawberries, hulled and sliced

Combine flour, pecans and butter; mix well. Press evenly on bottom of 13×9-inch pan. Bake in preheated 375° oven for about 20 minutes. Cool on wire rack.

Combine gelatin, pie filling mix and water in medium saucepan; blend well. Cook and stir over medium heat until mixture comes to a boil. Remove from heat and stir in strawberries. Let stand about 5 minutes. Pour over cooled crust. Chill until set, about 5 hours. Garnish, if desired.

CROWN JEWEL DESSERT

Makes 8 cups or 16 servings

1 package (4-serving size) JELL-O® Brand Cherry Flavor
    Gelatin
1 package (4-serving size) JELL-O® Brand Lemon Flavor
    Gelatin
1 package (4-serving size) JELL-O® Brand Orange Flavor
    Gelatin
4 cups boiling water
1½ cups cold water
1 package (4-serving size) JELL-O® Brand Orange-
    Pineapple Flavor Gelatin
¼ cup sugar
½ cup cold canned pineapple juice
1¾ cups thawed COOL WHIP® Non-Dairy Whipped Topping

CONTINUED

■ ■ ■

Dissolve cherry, lemon and orange flavor gelatins separately, using 1 cup of the boiling water for each flavor. Add ½ cup of the cold water to each flavor. Pour each flavor into its own 8-inch square pan. Chill until firm, about 4 hours. Cut into ½-inch cubes.

Dissolve orange-pineapple flavor gelatin and sugar in remaining 1 cup boiling water. Add pineapple juice. Chill until slightly thickened. Blend whipped topping into orange-pineapple flavor gelatin. Fold in gelatin cubes. Pour into 9-inch tube pan or 8-cup mold. Chill overnight or until firm. Unmold. Garnish with whipped topping, if desired.

STRAWBERRY BAVARIAN PIE

Makes one 9-inch pie

   1 package (4-serving size) JELL-O® Brand Strawberry
        Flavor Gelatin
 ¼ cup sugar
   1 cup boiling water
 ¼ cup cold water
   1 pint strawberries, hulled and halved
1¾ cups thawed COOL WHIP® Non-Dairy Whipped Topping
   1 baked 9-inch pie shell, cooled   CONTINUED

■ ■ ■

■ ■ ■

Dissolve gelatin and sugar in boiling water. Add cold water. Chill until thickened. Arrange strawberries in bottom of pie shell. With electric mixer at medium speed, beat thickened gelatin until fluffy, thick and about doubled in volume. Blend in 1 cup of the whipped topping. Chill until mixture mounds. Spoon over berries in pie shell. Chill about 4 hours. Garnish with remaining whipped topping and additional berries, if desired.

MOLDED CHEF'S SALAD

Makes about 6 cups or 10 to 12 servings

     2 packages (4-serving size) or 1 package (8-serving size)
        JELL-O® Brand Lemon Flavor Gelatin
  1½ teaspoons salt
     2 cups boiling water
  1½ cups cold water
     1 tablespoon vinegar
   ½ teaspoon Worcestershire sauce
   ⅛ teaspoon black pepper
     1 cup finely shredded lettuce
   ½ cup thin tomato wedges
   ½ cup finely shredded chicory or endive
   ¼ cup thinly sliced scallions
   ¼ cup thinly sliced radishes
     2 tablespoons thin strips green pepper
     1 tablespoon French dressing
   ½ cup slivered ham, tongue or veal
   ½ cup slivered Swiss cheese

Dissolve gelatin and salt in boiling water. Add cold water, vinegar, Worcestershire sauce and pepper. Chill until slightly thickened.

Meanwhile, combine vegetables and dressing; let stand about 20 minutes to marinate. Fold vegetables, ham and cheese into gelatin. Pour into 6-cup ring mold or individual molds. Chill until firm, about 4 hours. Unmold. Serve with crisp salad greens and mayonnaise, if desired.

■ ■ ■

■ ■ ■

Zuppa Inglese

Makes 6 servings

2 tablespoons slivered blanched almonds
1 package (4-serving size) JELL-O® Vanilla Flavor Pudding
   and Pie Filling
2¼ cups milk
¼ cup hot water
½ cup apricot or peach preserves
2 teaspoons rum extract
4 slices pound cake, cut into strips
1 tablespoon grated BAKER'S® GERMAN'S® Sweet
   Chocolate
Confectioners sugar

Toast almonds in shallow pan in preheated 350° oven for 3 to 5 minutes; set aside. Combine pudding mix and milk in medium saucepan. Cook and stir over medium heat until mixture comes to a full boil. Chill about 30 minutes. Blend water into preserves; add rum extract. Arrange cake strips evenly around side of 1-quart serving bowl and spoon apricot mixture over cake. Pour chilled pudding into cake-lined bowl. Chill thoroughly. Just before serving, sprinkle pudding with almonds, chocolate and confectioners sugar.

Frozen Fruit Salad

Makes 6 cups or 12 servings

1 package (4-serving size) JELL-O® Brand Strawberry
   Flavor Gelatin
1 cup boiling water
1 can (6 fluid ounces) frozen concentrated lemonade
3 cups thawed COOL WHIP® Non-Dairy Whipped Topping
1 can (16 ounces) sliced peaches, drained and chopped
1 can (8½ ounces) pear halves, drained and chopped

Completely dissolve gelatin in boiling water. Add lemonade and stir until melted. Chill until slightly thickened. Blend in whipped topping and fold in fruit. Pour into 9×5-inch loaf pan. Freeze until firm, about 4 hours. Remove from freezer about 30 minutes before serving. Unmold and slice.

■ ■ ■

INDEX

■ ■ ■

■ ■ ■

■ ■ ■

■ ■ ■